MW01002202

Exit $trategy:

Maximizing the Value

of Your Business

Thomas W. Lyons

Cape Coral, Florida

1726 SE 44th Terrace
Cape Coral, Florida 33904

Exit Strategy:
Maximizing the Value of Your Business

First Printing December 2003
Second Printing November 2005
Third Printing June 2008

ISBN 10: 0-9818004-0-8
ISBN 13: 978-0-9818004-0-0
Library of Congress Control Number: 2008929614
Printed In the U.S.A.

Faelon Partners, Ltd.
Thomas W. Lyons, President
4979 Olson Memorial Hwy. Suite 101
Golden Valley, Minnesota 55427
763-231-4200 Ext. 1

www.faelon.com

The contents of this book are intended to raise issues of a general nature for the
reader. The authors do not intend to address all issues that may arise for either
the seller of a business or the buyer of a business in a contemplated transaction.
In contemplating the purchase or sale of a business, advice should be sought
from competent professionals before undertaking such a transaction; including
certified public accountants, attorneys, financial advisers, tax specialists,
appraisers, business brokers and other resource area specialists to assist the reader. Every transaction contemplated by a person interested in selling or purchasing a business has unique facts that are impossible to anticipate in a book of this
nature. These transactions require the ability to imagine a wide variety of potential future situations and the skill to specify precise procedures for dealing with
each situation which could arise. The author and his contributing writers dis-
claim any liability whatsoever to the reader and discourage the reader from
undertaking any transaction without the assistance of competent, trained professionals.

Table of Contents

Foreword

By General Harry A. Sieben, Jr.

Tom Lyons and I have been friends and professional colleagues for almost 30 years. My law firm hired Tom when he left the Air Force in the mid 1970s; and several years later I attended his wedding as a friend. He is a man of upstanding character. He serves people with loyalty and integrity. I've always known him to be kind, selfless and optimistic.

Tom served as office administrator for my law firm Sieben, Grose & Von Holtum for 10 years, guiding my firm into the uncharted region of marketing and advertising our services. I worked daily with him as he oversaw the business side of the legal profession, managing our firm through a rapid growth cycle.

Tom served his country as a Sergeant in the Air Force in Vietnam. He enlisted because he felt that was the right thing to do. After his honorable discharge, he continued to serve in the Air National Guard.

As a Brigadier General in the Air National Guard and as Minnesota's Adjutant General in charge of all Minnesota military personnel, I believe the U.S. military is a special opportunity with much to teach young people. However, it was Tom Lyons who taught the military a thing or two about integrity.

Somebody once defined integrity as "the choices you make when nobody else is watching." Tom has integrity. He always tries to do the right thing, whether he benefits or not; that's just the way his mind works. He gets the job done, and done right.

Selling a business is a decisive event in a person's life. It is an emotional decision and difficult to accomplish correctly alone. In this book, Tom demystifies the process of selling a business. Yes, the process can be complex, but it doesn't have to be foreign and esoteric.

This is the first book I've seen on selling a business that promotes it in the correct way. That is, the best way for the seller to be fully represented by advisors and experts in their respective fields. Being a lawyer, I strongly advocate for professional representation.

It is my honor to write this foreword. Enjoy this book and you will know the man who wrote it and know that it is the best way to sell your business.

Harry A. Sieben, Jr.
August 2003

President, Sieben, Grose, Von Holtum & Carey, LTD
Adjutant General, Minnesota National Guard (Ret.)
Brigadier General, Minnesota Air National Guard (Ret.)
Speaker of the Minnesota House of Representatives (Ret.)

Author Forward

To The Third Edition

When I began this project I had no idea of the demand for this book's timeless teachings. Culture has conditioned us to think in a particular way; unfortunately, that way isn't always beneficial to a business owner.

Take "retirement" for example. Today's culture teaches us that we retire at age 65. I counsel people to retire when you have enough resources to support your lifestyle indefinitely. If you have enough money to retire at age 50, then do so; just make sure you know what you're going to do with the rest of your life.

Introducing such concepts into the life cycle of business ownership is what Exit Strategy is all about: Retirement; Planning an exit strategy; Preparation; Controlling the timing of your exit from business ownership; and Executing the selling process.

Raising awareness of these concepts in the minds of business owners is the mission of this book. And it is the infrastructure of how my mergers and acquisitions advisory firm, Faelon Partners, Ltd., serves its clientele. The concepts explained in this book are based on decades of personal experience in mergers and acquisitions.

In short, these time-honored concepts will help you maximize the value of your business and minimize the tax ramifications of its sale.

It has been gratifying to take this message across the country, and now to Europe. I am thankful for the many professional advisors who have promoted the book, and for the many business owners who have come to us to advise them on their exit strategies.

I hope this Third Edition helps many more business owners achieve their personal and professional objectives. We look forward to helping you develop your personal exit strategy.

Sincerely,

Thomas W. Lyons, President
Faelon Partners, Ltd.
www.faelon.com

Introduction

SOONER OR LATER, you, like every business owner, will need to transfer ownership of your business. Selling the business is the final part of your role in building it. For most business owners, this is an emotional and sometimes overwhelming event.

Like you, many business owners have built the company or owned it for years, even decades. You are at it night and day, 24/7 — thinking about the business, cultivating customer relationships, solving problems even while out to dinner with your family and in the middle of the night while your family sleeps. You eat it, drink it and sleep it. You live the business and it may define you more than you realize. It is no surprise, then, that selling the business is an emotional process.

It's also a complex process. There are financials to audit, profitability to demonstrate, operations to tighten, confidentiality to maintain, titles to transfer, a price to negotiate and much more. In addition, you must continue to operate the business during the process. The broad complexities will become even more apparent as you read on.

We understand the complexities and the emotions involved in selling a business. After all, we've helped hundreds of people sell their businesses, and we've learned something from every sale. We've also watched people make mistakes — which is one of the big reasons for writing this book. The more you know about the processes, the fewer mistakes you'll make when selling your business. Which means more money in your pocket.

The principles this book lays out generally apply to every business, because in the mergers and acquisitions (M&A) industry every seller should be represented by highly experienced and strategic-minded M&A professionals, including M&A or brokerage advisors, financial planners, estate planning attorneys, insightful and knowledgeable Certified Public Accountants (CPA) and transaction attorneys.

One group of owners that will be particularly interested in the process explained in this book is the "middle market." By middle market we mean businesses smaller than multinational corporations, yet larger than "Ma and Pa" businesses. Large corporations and small businesses have needs met through alternative channels. That leaves middle market business owners to figure it out alone.

The biggest challenge we see is that business owners are islands; you're out there by yourself, isolated. You do everything: buying inventory, pricing, sales, controlling expenses, resolving human relations issues. Simply put, you need help to sell your business and maximize the value while minimizing the tax ramifications. You need a guide. That guide is your M&A advisor.

The M&A Advisor

The M&A advisor helps you get ready to sell your business early, while you have control over the factors involved and have the time to maximize its value

While selling your business may be a daunting task, there is help available to guide you through the selling process. As a guide, an M&A advisor, sometimes referred to as a business broker, performs several roles in the selling process. In general, the M&A advisor can be seen as a facilitator who brings to the process many talents and experiences.

An experienced M&A advisor is essential to maximize the value you receive for your business, which is critical to completing the selling process. He or she looks at the big picture process of the sale while managing the details. When dealing with a qualified M&A advisor, you will have a sense that the sale is moving forward, that momentum is developing, that the parties to the deal are communicating, and that you are being professionally represented.

Generally, the M&A advisor markets your business to targeted buyers and major buyer groups so that you can remain focused on running it.

Specifically, the M&A advisor helps you assemble a team of professionals, including: a financial planner, an estate planning attorney, a CPA and a transaction or M&A attorney. Because each sale is different and each owner's needs vary, you may or may not choose to use each of the advisors outlined in this book. It ultimately is your decision whom to include. If you are unsure about which of the advisors you need, your M&A advisor can recommend professionals in each area of expertise whom you can interview to help you make informed decisions.

The M&A advisor educates you on the selling process, facilitates the collection of necessary documents and consults with your team when necessary. For example, he or she should negotiate the deal according to your team's strategy to minimize tax ramifications for you.

The M&A advisor guides you through "seller's remorse." Seller's remorse is a common and a normal part of the process. Careful guidance by the M&A advisor will help your through this period of panic, stress and doubt. Resolving those concerns quickly allows the selling process to move forward with decisiveness and vigor.

The M&A advisor provides practical advice about the timing of selling your business... he's a valued business advisor

The M&A advisor provides practical advice about the timing of selling your business. Perhaps, for example, with a few changes here and there, you can keep your business and still achieve the near-term lifestyle that you want. A preferred M&A advisor will tell you this even if it means foregoing an immediate engagement.

The M&A advisor is a valued team member just like the other professionals you've assembled to counsel you. The only difference is that while other professionals help you grow, operate and account for your business, the M&A advisor helps you sell it.

Above all else, the M&A advisor is your advocate. He or she will make sure that you understand the attorney's legalese and the CPA's recommendations. If you are uncertain or uncomfortable about any aspect of the process, he or she can ask the necessary questions for you to make informed decisions. The M&A advisor then is your guide through the process of selling your business.

The Seller

You have several responsibilities in the sale of your business. Key among them are: a good reason for selling, continued operation of the business through the selling process, and open representation or full disclosure.

How many times have you thought to yourself: "I just don't have enough time to do the things I want?"

Throughout the process, you are advised to run the business as if you are going to keep it for many years to come—not to let up on the process of managing it and to continue to do all of the things that have made your business successful over the years. This is not only good for you in the event the sale does not go through; it is also good for the buyer because your business has been managed properly during the selling process.

In the event you just want to test the market or assess valuation, the opportunity to complete the sale is slim to none. As you read this book you will begin to see that you get only one good chance to market and sell your business at maximum valuation. Testing the waters for valuation purposes usually backfires and ends up devaluing the business when you are finally serious about selling. Serious buyers will not spend the time and money to evaluate your business a second time.

Finally, full disclosure is a common term used in transactions. It is important for you to fully disclose all aspects of your business and your history at the business. If you perceive a problem, the M&A advisor can find someone to help you fix it. It may turn out to be minor or a non-issue. It's important to address all issues as early in the process as possible, because, as we'll see in a later chapter, the buyer's team of advisors will discover it. If dealt with early, then the issue may not affect the process.

Throughout the process, the seller is advised to run the business as if he or she is going to keep it for many years to come

Once a buyer steps forward, a period of due diligence ensues. During this period you are expected to "open the books and unlock the doors." The prospective buyer and his or her representatives must be given complete access to all aspects of your business. In return, you can expect complete confidentiality.

Key Steps and Time Frames for Successful Sales

The selling process can be complex; it takes time to put together the deal. While timelines vary from several months to several years, a typical process may take up to a year from the first discussion until closing.

The steps and timelines are listed on the next page.

Key Steps and Time Frames for Successful Sales

The successful sale of most companies generally follows predictable steps as listed below. Once you have retained your M&A advisor, these are the steps used to find and select the best possible buyer for your business.

Develop Marketing Strategy & Materials   **3-4 Weeks**
1) Discuss estate/tax planning
2) Assemble team, e.g., CPA, M&A attorney
3) Prepare Sales Information Book
4) Create buyer list/marketing strategy

Market Business for Sale   **6-8 Weeks**
1) Mail letters and business profile
   to prospective buyers
2) Follow up with telephone conferences
3) Evaluate and financially qualify buyers
4) Obtain signed confidentiality agreements
5) Send out sales information books

Screen Prospective Buyers   **6-8 Weeks**
1) Refine list of interested buyers
2) Receive and evaluate bids

Finalize Transaction   **8-12 Weeks**
1) Conduct management presentations
2) Assist in review of purchase agreements
3) Support due diligence process

Closing   **4-8 Weeks**
1) Assist with documentation to facilitate
   the closing of the transaction
2) Assist the seller with post-closing issues

Faelon Partners, Ltd. 763-231-4200 www.faelon.com

Retirement Planning

There are several good reasons to sell a business. Retirement is one of the most common. Today's culture teaches that retirement commences at age 65. However, we'd like you to consider a different definition. We encourage clients to think of retirement in terms of having enough money to sustain a chosen lifestyle indefinitely. If you have enough money to retire at age 50, then do so; just make sure you know what you're going to do with the rest of your life.

Everyone defines retirement differently. It is up to you to discuss investment strategies with your financial planner, and retirement lifestyle with your spouse. Your plan should include staying physically and mentally active, and engaged in fulfilling activities in order to enjoy a long and rewarding retirement.

Succession Planning

Like retirement planning, succession planning is such an important topic that we often ask buyers to consider it even before buying a business; and certainly well in advance of selling one. Succession planning involves answering several questions. Some of those questions are: Why are you buying the business? How long are you going to own it? How big do you want it to become? What are you going to do with it when you are ready to sell it? And there are still other questions that guide a business owner through the issues of succession planning, and serve to develop an effective exit strategy.

Business owners can choose from many different exit strategies such as transferring the company to family members; selling the business to one or more key employees; creating an Employee Stock Ownership Plan (ESOP); instituting an Employee Stock Purchase Plan; engaging in a public offering; liquidating the company; or selling the company to the buyer that is willing and able to pay the highest price for the business. Each of these succession plans will also be a part of your estate plan. (See: "Trusts & Estate Attorney")

Regardless of which method you choose to exit your company, this book will be helpful by walking you through the options available to you and showing you what is involved in the sale of your company. Many of the methods mentioned can be handled in an efficient manor with the help of your CPA and attorney or an attorney who specializes in ESOP's; however, as you will see, an experienced M&A advisor can be invaluable as your guide to selling your business and using the proceeds (money) to take care of your family and trusted employees.

Moving Forward

This book will explain the process of selling your business and why you need an experienced M&A advisor to guide you through that process. It's not intended to be a "do-it-yourself" book, because you shouldn't try to do it yourself. If you learn only one thing from this book it should be this: seek professional advice early, and rely on professionals during the process.

The process laid out in this book is full-service and broad-based. It's a process developed over a quarter century of experience in building, operating, buying and selling businesses. Because M&A advisors do not service their clients in the same way, it is important to discuss the engagement with your advisor in detail and require an engagement letter that states clearly what services will be performed and what fees will be charged.

If you do the things laid out in this book, you too will have the kind of professional representation that large corporations enjoy while selling your business without employing teams of attorneys and accountants. This book will describe the process and explain how, by contracting for the sale of your business with an experienced M&A advisor, you can rest easy and keep more of your money at the end of the process.

Whatever the deal looks like in the end, you will need to begin the selling process with careful preparation. ∎

1 | Preparing Your Business For Sale

WITH A LITTLE WORK, every business can be prepared and improved prior to its sale. A well-prepared business gets more offers, and usually better offers, than does a less-prepared one. A well-prepared business also advances the sale more quickly. Due diligence (See : "From the Buyer's Perspective") is less time-consuming, as there are fewer questions and more credibility in the eyes of the buyer.

Chances are your business can be improved in ways that enhance a buyer's confidence. The more comfort and trust the buyer has in you and your business, the fewer opportunities a buyer has to question various aspects of the business and negotiate a lower price.

In most cases, you should begin preparing your business for sale the day you buy it or open it. Since that day has passed, let's talk about what to do now to prepare for a future sale.

A Good Reason to Sell

As mentioned in the Introduction, one of your key responsibilities is to have a good reason to sell. The possibility of completing the sale of a business will be better if you are properly motivated.

What is a good reason to sell? The typical reasons that drive the selling process through to closing include:

- ▶ Retirement
- ▶ Ill health
- ▶ Too rapid growth
- ▶ Undercapitalization
- ▶ Lack of interested heirs
- ▶ Divorce
- ▶ Major or dramatic industry changes

Conflict within you can arise if you really want to keep the business but feel as though you're trapped into selling it. A good M&A advisor will press a little and offer solutions that may not involve selling.

For example:

One young owner wanted out. He was spending sunrise to sunset running his business. A buyer stepped forward and was ready to write a check. The seller asked us what we thought. We told him, don't sell. You're too young.

He was surprised. So we talked about some ideas that would allow him to spend less time at work. We made significant changes that led to a solution other than selling. He didn't know what his business was "supposed to" look like as it grows. So we worked on bookkeeping and general management. We helped him empower his employees to do more.

Today, he works 50 hours a week. He takes vacations. His business is growing and thriving. He has more than doubled revenues. He can sell his business in several years, when it's worth more money and he's more comfortable letting it go. And in the meantime, he's working on estate and financial planning to get ready.

Having a good reason for selling your company is the beginning of your preparation process. A thorough understanding of your motivation for selling will support an efficient and effective selling process and a more lucrative outcome for you.

Personal Preparation

Preparing your business for sale also means preparing yourself for life after the sale. This topic is so important and so commonly ignored in the M&A industry that we devoted an entire chapter to it (See: "After the Sale: What Then? Successful Retirement Requires Planning).

Rare is the person who sells his or her business and easily parts with it. Begin now to prepare yourself: When you sign on the dotted line, be ready.

Generally speaking, you will need to spend time considering the following questions:

▶ What is your business worth?

▶ How much is your real estate worth?

▶ How do you go about selling your business?

▶ What is the best way to define your business to position it for sale?

▶ What are the legal and accounting ramifications of the sale?

▶ What are the tax implications of the sale? How are you going to allocate the purchase price and how much does that mean you owe in federal and state income taxes?

▶ After you've paid taxes and your advisors, what's left for you?

▶ Is this really the time to sell?

▶ If it's not worth what you hoped it was, what should you do?

As you can see from these questions, preparing your business for sale is more than dusting the drill press and aligning the financials. Most of these questions, in a direct way, will affect your life during the selling process and long afterward.

When Should You Sell?

Now that you have a good reason to sell and you think you're well on your way to being prepared, it's time to ask when is the best time to sell? Should you sell now or wait for some life-changing event? As you begin to consider all the ramifications of selling now or later, you'll find yourself revisiting your personal preparation. Here's what we mean.

You will need to consult with your CPA, your family and especially your spouse about the timing of the sale. Your spouse will have strong feelings one way or another about the sale. In fact, often the spouse will need to attend the closing in order to sign certain legal documents.

Also, your life after the sale will affect your spouse. Your spouse may be thinking about long-term financial security and will have questions concerning that. The questions will raise important matters to discuss. A financial planner may be just the answer to such considerations.

These are difficult issues that affect your decision of when to sell the business. In addition to your CPA, your spouse and a financial planner, your M&A advisor is experienced in bringing together the professionals you may need to help you decide when to sell.

What Parts of the Business
Need Prepping?

Finally, you're prepared to sell the business and you've decided on the timing. You are ready to dive into the process now. So let's start preparing the business for the sale.

Every business can use some preparation for its sale. By preparation we mean bringing crisp and well-defined order to your financial statements, updating employee training, clarifying procedures and physically sprucing up the facility. The specifics on what needs to be done depend on an objective assessment of your business and its uniqueness.

Financials: Clean Up the *Financial Statements* To put it succinctly: clean financial records are a must. Any discrepancies or sloppiness in your financial statements reflect on the overall quality of the business and its operations. Get the financials in the best condition possible.

Simplify and clean up expenses. Keep costs directly related to the business. Anything unusual that shows up on the financials and is unnecessary to the operation of the business creates doubt in the mind of the buyer. This doubt, whether real or not, may detract from the value of the business.

In addition to keeping clean financial records, work hard to demonstrate steady growth, profitability and improving margins. This is referred to as the trend factor.

The Trend Factor Buyers like to see positive trends. Showing a multiyear trend of increasing revenue and profitability and a trend of lower cost of goods sold significantly heightens the buyer's interest in your business.

Increasing Gross Revenue and Profitability

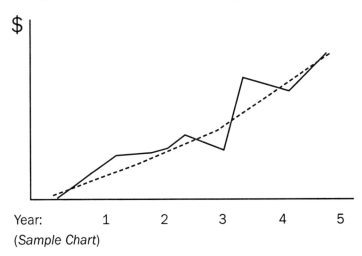

Year: 1   2   3   4   5
(*Sample Chart*)

Looking at the chart above, the buyer will be more interested in the trend represented by the straight line than in the dips and valleys of the actual gross revenue and profitability numbers. That is not to say the buyer will ignore the actual numbers; it is, however, to say that the trend may be more important to the buyer because it is an indicator of the potential to grow the business and operate it profitably.

Some other considerations that affect financial statements include customer diversification, certified audits and capitalization.

Diversify your customer base and increase overall numbers of customers. The more customers your revenue is spread across, the more valuable your business is, due to the fact that if you lose any single customer it will not hurt profitability as much.

Most businesses include some unnecessary expenses at the owner's discretion

Completing a certified audit may be beneficial. A certified audit can be expensive; however, it sends unambiguous messages of commitment to accuracy and confidence in your business to potential buyers.

Finally, invest in your company; invest in your growth. Keep enough money in the business to operate it efficiently and effectively. Even with your commitment to sell, keep the business growing and vital. That makes it more attractive to potential buyers.

The Management Team:
Key Hires

Another way to prepare your business for sale is to build an effective management team. Make sure that key people in your organization are as fully trained as possible to perform those important roles. Key employees include: CEO, COO, CFO and your sales management team.

Buyers want to see a good management team in place. That might include hiring someone to take your place in the daily operations of the business. The more experienced the team and the longer they've been together, the more valuable they are and the more likely they become an asset supporting the sale.

To mold your management team into a supporting asset, begin transferring duties and responsibilities to them. Transfer professional contacts and customer relationships. Show the buyer that your presence in the office is not necessary to the growth and profitability of your business. The buyer wants to be able to step in, replace you and continue to grow the business without interruption. To this end, it is common for a buyer to ask the current owner to remain for a set amount of time — six months to a year is typical.

The better your management team can run the business, the less time you will likely have to remain to support the buyer through the transition. The more thoroughly prepared they are to run the business, the more confidence a buyer will have in them and the sooner you can walk away from the business after selling it.

Train Employees

One of the first things a buyer asks about is the people. People, their experience, their responsibilities and their productivity are critical to the deal and the business' sustained profitability.

Poorly trained employees may be a hindrance to maximizing the value of your business; they provide the buyer with reasons to negotiate a lower price. On the other hand, investing in employees' professional development can improve productivity, increase profitability and increase the price a buyer is willing to pay for your business.

The better your employees are trained and prepared, the more valuable they are to a buyer and the more secure their positions will be with the new owner.

Systems and Procedures

Make sure a system exists for everything that happens in your business. And then be sure your employees are trained to follow them. Clarify procedures. Systematize tasks. Print manuals describing functions and operations. To the extent possible, write down everything that occurs in the operation of the business.

Well-defined and documented systems and procedures have multiple benefits for a business. They make operations run more efficiently and force better organization of the business. Well-defined safety systems and procedures typically lower insurance costs and create safer work environments and more productive employees.

Finally, document clearly what benefits employees receive. Help the buyer avoid potential pitfalls or confrontations; make sure the buyer knows all details and employee expectations upfront.

The better the buyer understands the "rules," the easier it will be to transition into a leadership role and manage the employees, and the easier it will be for you to walk away.

The buyer likes to see systems and procedures because they foster a better sense of how the business runs. They're reassuring, evoking a sense that fewer uncontrolled events and fewer surprises will occur. This comfort, or level of confidence, may result in a higher value for your business.

Real Estate

Also, well before the active search for a buyer begins, it is advisable to assess the status of your real estate. If it is owned, you will want to have title work completed. A title update is necessary to ensure that there are no glitches, such as inaccurate legal descriptions. Also, an up-to-date survey will be required.

> *In the process of selling one particular business, it was discovered during the title search that the legal description of the owned property was confusing. Further research revealed that the entire section, including the business' real estate, had been inaccurately surveyed by two feet, resulting in a long delay in the selling process.*

Investigate and clear any possible liens on the title, including mortgages, mechanics liens and any old or unresolved claims. If the title is transferred by a contract for deed, confirm that the contract has been filed and satisfied.

Whether you own or lease the real estate, order a Phase I Environmental Assessment. If the assessment shows any potential problems, you may be required to do further testing and even pay for any cleanup of waste, whether or not you caused the problem. We recommend consulting with your attorney on such matters.

The following is an example of commencing the assessment in the preparation stage of the selling process:

> *A seller did not want to do a Phase I Environmental Assessment until after a buyer was found. The result was a six-month delay in the closing because the study, once it eventually was completed, found several environmental issues, including: underground tanks, construction waste that had been dumped on the adjoining property and overflowed onto the seller's property, lead from the property's use by the local law enforcement agency as a firing range and the existence of some Indian burial grounds on the property. This land and business had been in the same family for decades and no one remembered all of the events that affected the property over the years. The deal could have been closed much more quickly if the seller had prepared the environmental study at the beginning of the selling process.*

Physical Facility

Cosmetic upgrades help the business appear well cared for. Clean, shine and paint old equipment. Mow the lawn! Clip the shrubs. Paint the building, foundation, shutters and trim.

Sell or throw out old equipment. If it no longer is a direct part of creating your products or running the business, then remove it from the facility and from the list of assets.

Summary

Preparing your business for sale is a process of decisions and action steps. These action steps are the first and the most immediate steps you can take in selling your business. The items discussed in this chapter establish a base from which you can determine an approximate valuation for your business.

To review, preparing your business for sale is a future-focused attempt to create the necessary trends that maximize the value of your business. Preparing your business for sale also encourages you to make a serious assessment of your financial statements and other legal documents, your management team and employees, and your systems, procedures and the status of your physical facility.

With proper motivation and planning, it will be possible to sell your business at its greatest value. ■

2|Business Valuation

YOU HAVE SEVERAL WAYS to value your business. There's the old "talking it over with a friend" method. Most buyers, however, are not going to put much credibility in your friend's numbers.

Another likely source for a business owner to derive the value of his or her business is a personal accountant. Tax returns, financial statements, depreciation schedules and other pertinent financial data will provide important information. You may want to retain your CPA to prepare a formal business evaluation.

> **When an M&A advisor is involved, buyers know the seller is serious about selling the business**

There are also numerous proverbial "rules of thumb." You've probably heard of many of them. However, they rarely answer the kinds of questions a buyer will ask, such as: "How many years will it take me to achieve my investment goals? And how many years will it take me to get a return of and on my investment?"

Let's debunk the myth now: There is no secret formula

that determines the value of your company. There are so many variables that a magic formula would be impossible to create.

In short, there are as many ways to value businesses as there are people to value them. An M&A advisor will value a business with an in-depth analysis of the practical part of the business that buyers want: They want to buy your assets and revenues.

Business valuation is based on the history of the business. Everything you do in preparation for selling your business directly impacts the value of it, such as those explained in the previous chapter.

> You get one good opportunity to market your business and achieve the highest price for it; rarely does a second chance present itself

Establishing a reasonable value for your business is critical. An unreasonably high valuation will raise serious questions in the minds of the buyers about the credibility of the sale and ultimately chase them away. You get one good opportunity to market your business and achieve the highest price for it; rarely does a second chance present itself. Professional buyers know the industry and common valuations; they know what's reasonable and what's not.

Conversely, offering a business at a low valuation prohibits raising the price at a later date. The result is receiving less money than what the business is actually worth.

The best course of action determines a reasonable price justified by assets being sold and the profitability of the business. And then, build in a premium to allow for the negotiating process. This strategy will help you reach the best possible purchase price.

What do you think your business is worth?

So, what is your business worth? And how do you go about determining the business valuation?

Looking at your business valuation critically may be difficult. Emotionally, most business owners believe their businesses are worth more than they are. This is one example of how selling a business is an emotional experience. You must come to terms with the fair market value of your business.

Your M&A advisor can facilitate the valuation process. Many variables, both quantifiable and intangible, are considered. Of all the possible variables, your business valuation should consider the following:

- ▸ Multiple of earnings value, including an indication of the owner's discretionary cash flow
- ▸ Asset valuation, including real estate, tangible and intangible assets
- ▸ A comparison of value to other businesses in the industry

Multiple of Earnings Value (Owner's Discretionary Cash Flow)

A buyer will want to know how much money a business makes after the expenses of operating the business. In order to communicate this on a universally accepted basis, most accountants refer to the EBITDA number as a good measure of the profitability of the business. EBITDA means earnings before interest, taxes, depreciation and amortization.

This number can be calculated from your income and expense statement by adding up:

	Net income after taxes
+	Interest expense
+	Income taxes
+	Depreciation
+	Amortization
	EBITDA

Your M&A advisor will start with the EBITDA calculation and add to it any expenses of a discretionary nature to come up with what is commonly referred to as the owner's discretionary cash flow. This represents the cash the business produces that is available to an owner (seller or buyer) to use at their discretion, including the payment of: debt service, owner's salary, company vehicle, insurance, or any other expenses of a discretionary nature.

M&A advisors may use owner's discretionary cash flow to help substantiate the best possible value of the business. This is the number that may then be used to calculate the approximate value of your business after factoring in suitable multiples for your industry.

Asset Valuation

Another approach commonly used to value your business is the asset valuation method. In order to use this method you would review your balance sheet and place a fair market value on all of the assets used in the operation of your company. You would assign these values to your furniture, fixtures, equipment, inventory, investments, real estate, intangible assets and any other assets owned by the business. Intangible assets would include any trademarks, patents and the value of goodwill.

Real Estate

Whether you own or lease, you must deal with real estate. You will need to establish the value of owned land and buildings. In the end, you may or may not include real estate in the sale, but for purposes of valuation, you need to provide the buyer with a complete physical and financial understanding of your business. That includes real estate.

Typically, whether or not real estate is included in the sale depends on the tax implications and financial planning strategies. It may be to your advantage to sell the real estate outright along with your business, or you may be better off leasing it now and selling later. An analysis of the tax implications with your advisors will help establish your goals.

Remember, the buyer's interest may conflict with your interest regarding the sale or retention of real estate. Remaining open to other possibilities will help facilitate the closing of a deal that is good for you and the buyer.

Furniture, Fixtures, Equipment and Inventory Equipment is most valuable as it relates to the income stream it produces for a growing business. In other words, while these assets are important, their importance is relative to the income they help to generate. As such, their value to your business is not necessarily based on their cost (as accounted for in depreciation schedules). Rather, their value is confirmed by their function in a profitable business operation.

Because accounting for such assets depends on the structure of the deal and the allocation of the purchase price, which are decisions generated by you and your CPA, we will return to assets in chapter eight.

That said, your business owns things such as computers, desks, chairs and other equipment. Your business valuation must include such items. A complete listing of them and their approximate value will be important to the buyer.

Only assets that allow you to produce income are important to the buyer

Goodwill or Intangible Asset Values The final part of the valuation is the goodwill or intangible asset value. This value can best be explained by asking the following questions:

▸ How much is the relationship you personally have with your largest customer worth?

▸ How much is your brand worth?

▸ How much are your intangible assets, such as patents and copyrights, worth?

▶   How valuable is your growth potential?

These are difficult questions to answer. Take a famous brand such as Coca Cola as an example. How much is the Coke brand worth? How do you quantify it?

Goodwill is the non-asset, profit-making infrastructure that you, as owner, created. It includes: reputation, relationships, service, customer lists and telephone numbers, among others. It's the premium that's paid for the business. For example:

> If you have $7 million in assets, and sell the business for $8 million, the difference is the goodwill value.

There is no objective measure by which to value intangible assets. It is the job of the M&A advisor to facilitate your assessment of goodwill values in such a way that it won't chase away would-be buyers.

Nobody knows your business as intimately as you do. So, ask yourself this question: "How much would I pay for my business?" The difference in the price and the asset value is a good starting point in assessing goodwill value.

If this is only a starting point in assessing goodwill value, then what are some of the other aspects of the assessment?

One aspect of the assessment is the buyer's investment timeline. The buyer will assess a goodwill value relative to the number of years it takes to get the investment returned and make money on it. If the buyer's investment timeline is five to seven years, and the seller's goodwill value places the total cost of the business within the timeline, then the buyer may accept the value. The timeline will differ with each buyer.

Another aspect is terms. If as a part of the purchase price you are willing to participate in the profits going forward (via an earn-out), then that may allow a buyer to pay more and allocate the premium to goodwill.

Comparable Value

If available, the price for which a comparable business in your industry sold will help establish the value of your business. Remember, every business is unique and your business will not sell for the exact price as one similar to it. However, it may give you an idea of your industry's typical multiplier for use in the multiple of earnings method of valuation explained earlier in this chapter.

Any doubts in the buyer's mind lowers the price he or she is willing to pay

Summary

To calculate a business' value, we use a combination of three methods: multiple of earnings, asset value, and comparable value. The calculations will produce approximate valuations. An average of these three methods may produce the best indication of value for your business.

To put that range in context, we can evaluate it by answering three questions. Given the valuation, if the business continues to operate the way it is currently:

▸ How many years will it take the buyer to get a return of the investment (down payment)?

▸ How many years will it take the buyer to get a return on the investment (ROI)?

▸ How many years will it take the buyer to repay the balance of the acquisition debt?

If the answers come out to be between five and seven years (the typical buyer's expectation for a return on investment), then the valuation range may be one to take to the market. If done right, you will have multiple buyers with competing prices within the range.

Remember from the beginning of this chapter, the goal is to calculate a fair market value. Valuations that are too high will not attract serious buyers; valuations that are too low will not provide you with enough money for your business. Bringing an appropriate valuation to the market is the most accurate and effective way to fairly present your business. ∎

3 | Assembling and Managing the Team of Advisors

THROUGH THE PREPARATION and business valuation process-es, the complexity of selling your business begins to emerge. Some sellers start to get overwhelmed at this point. Understandably so: there are many things to assess and consider.

To deal with these issues, you will want to assemble a team of professionals whose contributions meet your personal financial and legal needs and contribute to the selling process. If you do not have access to professionals experienced in mergers and acquisitions, your M&A advisor can provide recommendations. The team necessary to properly sell a business may include: the M&A advisor, a personal financial planner, an estate planning attorney, a CPA and a transaction attorney.

The team's roles in the process must be managed in order to maximize its contributions without accruing unnecessary fees in the process of completing the deal. In fact, the roles of your team's members can easily overlap if not managed properly. Clearly defined roles and responsibilities will result in the elimination of duplicate efforts, lower professional fees and a more efficient selling process.

You should be proactive in voicing your opinions and ensuring that your team acts in a timely and efficient manner. Team members should present their opinions and recommendations to you, allow you to make decisions and then complete the sale at your instruction without delay.

Of course, this is a large responsibility for you to manage while also running your business. To ease this responsibility, your M&A advisor should be adept at managing your team of advisors.

The Quarterback

Every team needs a quarterback, a leader to oversee functions and ensure that the team is moving toward the common goal—in this case, selling your business. The quarterback leading your team of advisors is the M&A advisor.

The M&A advisor is the most active of the team's memebrs because the he or she oversees the process of selling the business. The process involves:

- ▸ Coordinating the personal financial planning and estate tax strategy
- ▸ Helping establish a business valuation
- ▸ Preparing the business profile
- ▸ Identifying possible buyers
- ▸ Marketing the business for sale
- ▸ Negotiating the sale
- ▸ Monitoring the tax and legal ramifications with advice from the CPA and transaction attorney
- ▸ Facilitating the preparation of the purchase agreement and other documents to make sure the closing takes place in a timely fashion.

Working on your behalf, the M&A advisor ensures that critical ques-

The M&A advisor serves by guiding you through the process and ensuring that you understand what is happening at every stage

tions are asked and that answers match the nature of your wishes. Your advisor should ask your CPA questions about every aspect of the deal to make sure that you understand all the details and ramifications of the sale, and the options available to you.

The M&A advisor also facilitates legal explanations of the purchase agreement from the transaction attorney. If the attorney is not explaining the agreements in a way that you understand, then your M&A advisor must be aware and experienced enough to intercede to assist the discussion. To put it bluntly, if your eyes gloss over, if you begin to stray, then the attorney is speaking in too much legalese and your M&A advisor may need to step in on your behalf and ask for an explanation in simple English. Most attorneys are sensitive to this issue and careful to communicate clearly with their clients.

The financial planner, estate planning attorney, CPA and transaction attorney all work for you. They should present all selling options to you and let you make the decision that is best for you. The M&A advisor can help ensure that your wishes are followed.

Drafting the Team

Once the decision has been made to start the process of selling your business and you have selected the M&A advisor that you want to work with, it is time to determine what other help and advice you will need to make the best possible decisions during the selling process. As you will read in later chapters, the sooner you create a personal financial and estate planning strategy, the more likely it is that the sale of your business will meet your goals. We recommend creating such strategies as far in advance of the sale as possible. Chapters Four and Five will explain why this is critical.

You will need to determine whether or not you require the help of a financial planner. You will also want to consult with an experienced estate planning attorney to determine whether or not anything can be done to minimize the estate and gift tax ramifications of selling your business. This will be different for every business owner depending on the size of the business to be sold, the amount of other assets owned and the choices you make on behalf of your family. Once these issues are in order, the process of selling your business can commence.

At this point you will need to determine who will be guiding you through the income-tax ramifications of the sale and who will be examining and preparing the legal documents related to the sale.

You can include current advisors with whom you may work on the advisory team. You control which of the advisors you want involved in the process of selling your business. However, we strongly recommend that you consult with someone in each of the professions referred to in this book, even if in the end you decide not to utilize one or more of them.

This coordinated approach invariably has transitional areas among the advisors. They all have expertise; usually two and sometimes three of them will be attorneys. They are usually knowledgeable and experienced people and their advice may reduce the number of obstacles you will encounter during the sale of your business.

The following is a list of the advisors and a general summary of their respective roles:

Financial Planner Financial planners are experts in strategizing your personal finances and managing your personal risk exposure. They help you determine how many assets you will need to generate the level of income you desire to successfully meet your retirement objectives. In doing so, they are critical in determining the proper timing of the sale of your business. (See: "The Personal Financial Planner")

Trusts and Estate Attorney Trusts and estate attorneys are experts in structuring your estate to conform to tax law. They help clients create appropriate gifting strategies. They also create wills, trusts and other estate planning documents. By structuring an estate in a strategic manner, it serves the client's current financial needs and those of the recipients of the estate assets and can minimize estate and gift taxes. (See: "Trusts and Estate Attorney")

Accountant (CPA)   CPAs prepare formal financial statements and interpret what they mean for running and selling a business. Your CPA plays a key role in structuring the sale of your business and in maximizing net profit from the sale after payment of income taxes and fees. (See: "Your Accountant")

Transaction Attorney   M&A attorneys are experts in the language of the deal; a successful sale cannot occur without an experienced attorney. While the bulk of the work for the attorney comes near the end of the process, the M&A advisor should keep all team members informed from the beginning with phone calls, notes and copies of critical documents. The attorney's input along the way will be important. (See: "The Transaction Attorney")

An M&A advisor along with a team of professional advisors will give you the greatest opportunity to make informed decisions throughout the selling process. And the broker will work to ensure that the advisors present all options available to you. By using a team to help you make critical decisions about the sale of your business, you can maximize the amount of money a buyer is willing to pay and minimize tax ramifications on the sale. At the same time, you take comfort in knowing that your personal finances are in order, your estate has been organized and your business has been properly sold.

This book discusses each of the advisors and their roles in detail. The first, starting with the next chapter, is the personal financial planner. ■

4|The Personal Financial Planner

THIS CHAPTER WAS WRITTEN with generous contributions of time and expertise by Charles J. Maxwell, Jr.

Charles J. Maxwell, Jr., CFP is Chairman and Chief Executive Officer of Meristem, a multi-family office located in Minnetonka Minnesota. Meristem, formerly The Sage Partnership, serves over 100 families in 33 states and 8 countries. Mr. Maxwell's areas of wealth management expertise include investment advisory services, estate planning and business succession planning. Mr. Maxwell is the father of triplets. He says: "Wealth's true value is brilliantly clear. An exceptional awareness of astute planning is essential with triplets. And multitasking is definitely not a problem."

Of the professionals you will need to advise you on the sale of your business, the financial planner is the most personal. Financial planning encompasses your entire life, so the sale of your business will be a critical financial milestone.

Your financial planner needs to understand your current financial situation and assess the impact of the sale so that your exit strategy is well positioned. Your financial planner will discuss with you the reality of the net-after-tax financial world and what that means to your lifestyle. He or she should address the need to make sure that your level of replacement income supports your lifestyle. In other words, prior to the sale you and your planner need to quantify your financial picture in the post-sale world and develop a forward-looking picture of your financial situation.

Getting Your Financial Planner Involved Early

The sooner your financial planner knows your intention to sell the business, the better. This point can't be overstated. You should implement your pre-sale financial strategy as far in advance of the sale of your business as possible. This gives you and your planner more options to develop comprehensive planning and sales strategies.

Some business owners think that financial planning begins about a month before the sale; or after the transaction is in place. Once all the documents have been drafted and the only thing left to do is close the deal, you've lost your opportunity to maximize a planning strategy.

Some sellers become so eager to complete the sale that the rapidity of the transaction prevents them from implementing several pre-sale planning techniques that can benefit them from a financial and tax standpoint.

You will be able to work on the plan after the sale. However, some planning techniques such as estate planning and charitable trusts that are available pre-sale may no longer be viable if implemented after the sale.

Long-term strategies tend to lessen the impact of obstacles and surprises that emerge during the selling process. By coming to the M&A advisor and financial planner prior to selling the business, you may be able to work through a tremendous number of sale issues, including the tax and financial implications. A properly structured pre-sale financial and tax strategy may save you a significant amount of money depending upon the size and complexity of the transaction.

Selecting a Financial Planner

Finding the best financial planner is a critical decision for any individual. While a definitive checklist doesn't exist, there are indicators that can lead to the right planner for you.

Make certain that your planner is experienced and can demonstrate this to you. You should make sure that the planner is competent in the type of work you seek and has clients with similar net-worth issues. Education is important; and in the advisory field, so is experience.

Look for a financial planner who has owned or owns a business. The issues surrounding the sale of your business are deeper and more complex than doing an asset allocation pie chart, creating a budgeting graph or buying an insurance policy.

Also it is important to find a pragmatic and levelheaded advisor; someone whom you think has made good personal decisions.

Most competent advisors obtain their new clients from referrals by satisfied clients and other advisors who have witnessed their work. Asking your trusted advisors for referrals may be the best way for you to meet a competent certified financial planner.

Make certain that you have an engagement contract or a letter outlining the services to be rendered, the fee arrangement and the frequency of communications you may expect. Ask the planner to prepare meeting agendas or outlines, to make sure your important issues are being addressed.

Beginning the Planning Process

Here's an instructive scenario:

Someone walks into your office and makes an offer to buy your business. It's a big, flattering number. You have visions of no more risk and anxiety. That lifestyle you dreamed about involving beaches, travel and golf suddenly seems within reach. All sorts of thoughts and feelings are put in motion. The question is: Do you sell?

That's a compelling situation. But selling may not be the right thing for you to do. Some questions need to be asked to clarify your motivation.

This is when your professional advisors become more than just an M&A advisor and financial planner. They must go beyond the fee-based transaction mindset and into your life and understand what you really want and who you really are. Sometimes an owner thinks that selling is the only option when really there are alternatives. Depending on your lifestyle needs and your professional goals, you may not have to sell at this time.

One way to begin is to consider this question: What would need to happen in your world in the next three years to achieve all the objectives defined by your financial plan. If you can paint that picture, then you can work backward and make it happen.

Your M&A advisor and your financial planner should make sure these questions are answered:

▸ Are you depending on your business for lifestyle income needs?
▸ How much is your business worth?
▸ How much money will you have after the sale and payment of taxes and fees?
▸ Do you know where and how to invest your post-sale assets to protect them and guarantee income?
▸ Are you going to be able to live comfortably off the proceeds from the sale?

So, in some manner the financial planning process begins with understanding your motivation. No less important are your financial goals, and they are usually defined by personal needs and wants after the sale.

Objectives and Goal-Setting First, you will need to state some objectives and goals. Along with consulting your financial planner and estate planning attorney (for more detail on estate tax planning, see "Trusts and Estate Attorney"), you have to ask yourself: "Do I have the financial resources without the business to live the lifestyle I want?"

You will have to answer other questions, such as: Do you want to work? Do you want to travel? Where do you want to live? Healthcare needs? Insurance? How much money does that take? Some business owners have given this thought but, because they've been so busy running their businesses, they haven't committed it to paper and acted on the details. The personal financial planner will help you put the plan on paper and then will implement it for you. For example:

> An owner of a $10 million business takes out $600,000 in lifestyle expenditures such as travel, golf, car, auto insurance, cell phone and other perks. He decides one day to sell his business and nets $6 million on the sale. Assuming a low earnings rate of 5 percent, his $6 million earns him $300,000 per year pre-tax. That does not pay for the lifestyle he enjoys while owning the business. Without other assets to make up the difference or substantially reduced obligations, he may have to significantly change his lifestyle.

You must think critically and with advice about your future financial status and bring those financial goals to your advisors. They can help you analyze the salability of the business relative to your personal financial goals, or design the deal in such a way that you maintain certain privileges.

If the answer to the question of adequate financial resources to fund your lifestyle is no, then either you sell the business and get into something else, or don't sell yet.

Once you have your personal financial strategy and estate tax strategy in hand, the M&A advisor can move the process into the transaction phase, where other advisors work to structure the sale according to those objectives and goals.

Finances

Finally, a financial planner will assess your finances. The fundamental question financial planning deals with is: How do you achieve financial independence?

Sophisticated models can show how assets support your lifestyle goals. Financial planners can help you to build a model to suit your choices. The amount of assets from which you will derive your after-sale income depends on the proceeds from the sale of the business and other assets you've accumulated to date.

Review the Current Financial Plan

In working toward a financial strategy that recognizes and includes the ramifications of selling your business, your financial planner should review your current financial plan.

The review should include a reexamination of:

Assets and Investment Strategy   Is the asset base and investment strategy sound? Can they provide enough income to meet your retirement goals?

Estate and Gift Strategy   Financial and estate tax planners work hand in hand to create a strategy tailored specifically to the individual. Who and what are important to you? Spouse, children, grandchildren?

Risk Management   Liabilities such as those listed below must be accounted for in the financial plan.

- ▶ Warranties and Representations from the sale of the business
- ▶ "Tail" insurance coverage for exposures remaining from the business
- ▶ Property and Casualty liabilities
- ▶ Directors and Officers insurance
- ▶ Life, Health and Disability insurance
- ▶ Long-Term Care

If you leave employment, what do you do about health insurance or disability insurance?

How do you recover from a lost benefits menu?

You have to either insure the risk or assume the risk. If you're not associated with a group, insurance costs can be expensive. For example, if you drove a company car and will drive a personal car after the sale, you'll be responsible for car insurance. If you continue to sit on any boards, umbrella liability and directors and officers insurance may be at your personal expense after the sale.

If addressed prior to the sale, these issues could be accounted for in the structure of the sale and the allocation of its price (see Chapter Nine). The M&A advisor and your team should make sure that your liability exposures have been addressed in full and without any surprise gaps in coverage.

Opportunistic Pre-Sale Strategy

There are many pre-sale strategies that you can utilize to maximize the amount of gifts and charitable contributions you would like to make and to minimize transfer taxes. While this topic is more thoroughly discussed in the next chapter, it is important to understand that these pre-sale decisions may have a great impact on your financial strategy and tax liability post-sale.

Examples of Pre-Sale Decisions

A few techniques are listed below:

▸ Deferred compensation and consulting arrangements
▸ Continuation of income stream and benefit plans
▸ Reorganization of current portfolio of investment assets
▸ Tax loss harvesting in anticipation of gain from sale of the business
▸ Repositioning assets to generate income
▸ Preservation of assets (risk assessment)

These types of decisions will be impacted by your personal beliefs and financial planning strategies. For example:

> *Let's assume a person had a significant equity portfolio, even after turbulent markets. The current value is $3 million; the original cost basis was $4 million. In other words, there is a million dollars of losses tied up in your portfolio. If you know you are going to sell your business for a large taxable profit at the end of the year, you may want to sell the stocks and take the loss on paper, so that you can balance some of the gain from the sale of the business against the losses and reposition the assets.*

There are a lot of tricky issues that might be handled best by adding an experienced and knowledgeable financial planner to your advisory team.

In addition to the financial planner, you may want to discuss estate planning with an trusts and estate attorney as discussed in the next chapter. ■

5 | The Trusts and Estate Attorney

THIS CHAPTER WAS WRITTEN with generous contributions of time and expertise by Christopher B. Hunt.

Christopher B. Hunt, JD, is a shareholder in Fredrikson & Byron's Estate Planning service area. The emphasis of his practice is in estate planning, business succession planning, probate and related areas of real estate and property law. Mr. Hunt also handles a wide variety of business and tax planning work for clients, including charitable planning and dealing with the special estate planning problems of owners of closely held businesses.

It may seem an unusual proposition. But, when one is considering the sale of a business, it may be prudent to include a trusts and estate attorney among the team of professionals with whom the seller consults. By including a trusts and estate attorney in the process early enough, significant results can be obtained in a transfer of wealth to both family members and charitable organizations on a tax-advantage basis. In this chapter, we will introduce various transfer techniques to achieve both family estate planning and charitable objectives through both outright gifts and gifts through the use of trusts.

Getting Started

In order to begin the process, the business owner must make several different assessments. These include: 1) taking an inventory of the value and ownership of personal assets; 2) determining what other documents are in place, including other wills and trust agreements, buy/sell instruments or other agreements which restrict the transferability of business interests; and 3) determining the goals and objectives which apply to the situation.

This information-gathering process is critical to the overall success of the business owner's planning. The earlier that this process begins and the more complete its development, the more successful the various planning steps are likely to be.

Nature and Extent Completing an inventory of personal
of Assets assets includes listing a description of
each asset and its approximate value
and any encumbrances on the asset. It also includes a determination of how the asset is owned. That is, is it owned only in the business owner's name or are there other owners as well?

For many married business owners, this step reveals that the business owner owns the majority of the family's assets. One issue that your attorney will look at early on in the process is what steps can be taken to reallocate ownership of assets to the other spouse. This process may be affected by existing buy/sell arrangements or other restrictive agreements affecting the transferability of business interests. However, even in cases where such agreements are in place, there may be other assets that can be transferred between the spouses to create some relative balance between the estates.

Another common issue revealed during this stage is that the beneficiary designations may be incorrectly established. Often, the beneficiary designations are inconsistent with other estate planning documents. Another common mistake is to designate a beneficiary, who under law, cannot receive the benefits directly. The most common example of this would be to name a minor child as the beneficiary of retirement assets or life insurance proceeds.

Buy/Sell Documents   The business owner must also gather any existing buy/sell agreements or other instruments that may restrict the free transferability of business interests. Often, these agreements, which may have been in place for many years, are overlooked in the planning process. However, these documents can affect both the estate planning and business sale processes.

If the business owner is charitably minded and charitable trusts are used, the business interest must be transferred to the trust free of any restrictive agreements.

In these situations, written amendments to the agreements must be put into place before any transfer of the business interests can occur. The sooner these steps can occur, the better.

Goals and Objectives   Perhaps the most important phase in this initial estate planning process is the development of the business owner and spouse's goals and objectives. Business owners may determine that the amount of assets to be realized on the sale of their business will provide a comfortable retirement, but that there may not be substantial other assets in place which could be transferred to other members of the family or to charities. Other owners may decide that the sale proceeds will be more than enough to address their own needs and they may begin to look at what they would like to accomplish for other members of their family or charities.

In some cases, a business owner who has been very successful is faced with the decision of how much should be given to children or other members of the family. That is, even in cases where there is substantial wealth, are there limits on the amount that the business owner (and spouse) believes should be prudently transferred to members of the family or to trusts for their benefit?

As the goals and objectives are developed, the trusts and estate attorney can use this information to devise various strategies to fit the situation. Where appropriate, these strategies are often leveraged to produce the best tax results as well. The earlier that this process begins in relation to the sale of a business, the more likely a successful result will be obtained.

The following materials are designed to provide the business owner and spouse a summary of some of the key estate planning techniques used in connection with the sale of a business. It is important, however, for a reader to understand that this is not meant to be an exhaustive list of all the possible techniques or an in-depth description of each technique appearing here. However, this discussion is intended to facilitate a decision-making process and help you get started along that road. Consult with your attorney about your individual estate-planning situation.

Gifts
At the heart of any wealth transfer process is the annual exclusion gift. An annual exclusion gift is one where the donor intends to make a transfer of a "present interest" in property to one or more individuals. A present interest is one over which the recipient has immediate control. As an example, if the donor provides the recipient with $10,000 cash on which there are no restrictions, the gift is one of a present interest. On the other hand, if the donor provided the recipient with funds subject to a restriction that would not terminate for two years, the gift would be one of a "future interest" and would not qualify for the federal gift tax annual exclusion.

Under prior federal gift tax law, the federal gift tax annual exclusion was limited to $10,000 per year per recipient. Since 1998, the law recognizes a cost of living adjustment. For 2005, the annual exclusion amount was $11,000 per recipient. Your attorney can give you the current annual exclusion amount.

Under federal tax law, if a donor makes cumulative gifts in excess of the annual exclusion, a federal gift tax would be imposed. However, the donor would then be required to use a portion or all of the donor's available applicable exclusion amount against the gift tax. Under the law, which existed immediately prior to the federal tax changes made in 2001, the applicable exclusion (i.e., the amount which passes free of transfer tax after applying the taxpayer's unified credit) was slated to increase gradually between the amount of $600,000 and $1,000,000 by the year 2006.

Under 2001-tax legislation, the limits were increased to $1,000,000 in the year 2002. This amount is increased in three steps, to a maximum of $3,500,000 by the year 2009. While these amounts were increased rather dramatically, the overall limit for making gifts without a transfer tax was set at a maximum of $1,000,000. Even during 2010 when the federal estate tax is scheduled for repeal, the $1,000,000 limit on gifts without tax remains in place.

Gift-Splitting   A married couple can take advantage of a technique called "gift-splitting. Under the gift-splitting technique, each spouse is treated as if they had made one-half of the total gifts to an individual, even where the transfer of all of the assets has been made by only one spouse.

> EXAMPLE: *George makes a transfer of $22,000.00 of closely held stock to his son, Tim. As a result, there would be a taxable gift of $11,000.00. However, if George's spouse, Shirley, who has made no other gifts to Tim during the year, consents to gift-split, the gifts to Tim would not be taxable (assuming the present annual exclusion limit is at least $11,000).*

In order to avail themselves of the gift-splitting opportunity, the married couple must file a federal gift tax return on which the gift-splitting election is made.

In addition to the federal gift tax annual exclusion transfer, spouses themselves can transfer unlimited amounts between themselves without a gift tax, so long as certain conditions are met. This becomes an important issue when one spouse owns the majority of the assets (e.g., all of the stock in the company to be sold). Often, a realignment of the ownership of assets is beneficial when using some of the planning techniques described below.

Trusts   In many instances, the recipient of the gift is not ready for full control of the assets. A common example is where the recipient of the intended gift is a minor. In such instances, a trust could be created to hold the assets for the benefit of such a beneficiary until the beneficiary attains a more suitable age for management of the assets. In the meantime, the trustee, who has legal responsibility for the management of the trust assets, can utilize the assets for the benefit of the beneficiary. Within the trust instrument itself, one would specify how the assets are to be administered and distributed for the benefit of the beneficiary. This would include provisions which direct the trustee to distribute assets to the beneficiary under certain conditions or when the beneficiary has attained certain ages.

When trusts are used in conjunction with gifting, they must be made irrevocable. An irrevocable trust is one that cannot be amended or revoked after it has been created. Such a trust must be used in this situation so that the transfer will be treated as a completed gift for federal gift tax purposes.

Gifts for Descendants In Trust   There are many variations of trusts which are used in this situation. Where gifts are made for the benefit of children or other descendants, several common variations are: a Section 2503(c) trust, a trust containing Crummey withdrawal powers, a charitable remainder trust, a Grantor Retained Annuity Trusts (GRAT) and a generation-skipping trust.

For the purposes of this book, we will introduce an Irrevocable Trust containing Crummey withdrawal powers, a GRAT and a generation-skipping trust. For more information on other trusts, visit with your attorney.

Use of trusts to make gifts to beneficiaries that are intended to be subject to limitations is a common technique. Often an owner of a business will transfer interests in the business to trusts for the benefit of children or other descendants, so that the benefits of such a gift are realized in the future when the beneficiary is older and much better able to handle decisions regarding the use of such assets.

Irrevocable Trusts Containing Crummey Withdrawal Powers. A common type of trust used in connection with gifting, especially to minor beneficiaries, is a trust containing "Crummey" withdrawal powers. As gifts are made to the trust, the beneficiary will not have control over the assets until a later time. Consequently, these gifts to the trust will not qualify for the federal gift tax annual exclusion. This is due to the fact that the contributions do not qualify as a gift of a "present interest." However, if the trust contains Crummey withdrawal powers, contributions can qualify for annual exclusion treatment.

A typical Crummey withdrawal power permits the beneficiary, or the guardian or conservator of a minor beneficiary, a limited time after a contribution has been made to the trust, to withdraw the assets up to the value of the gift or the amount of the federal gift tax annual exclusion (or twice the annual exclusion for a married donor where gift-splitting is available), whichever is less. In order for the Crummey withdrawal power to be effective, the beneficiary must be notified of his or her rights to make such a withdrawal, including how to make such a withdrawal. Without notice to the beneficiary of this right, the withdrawal powers are ineffective to qualify the contribution for the federal gift tax annual exclusion.

Using a trust to make gifts to beneficiaries that are intended to be subject to limitations is a common technique. Future distributions from this type of trust can be made subject to any set of rules so long as the trust itself does not last longer than limits created under applicable state law. Often an owner of a business will transfer interests in the business to trusts for the benefit of children or other descendants, so that the benefits of such a gift are realized in the future when the beneficiary is older and much better able to handle decisions regarding the use of such assets.

Grantor Retained Annuity Trusts ("GRAT"). A GRAT is designed to make a gift of the remainder interest in property in trust. The person who creates such a trust, referred to as the "grantor," retains an annuity payment from the trust for a specific period of time. The remainder of the trust is transferred to the grantor's children or retained in trust for their benefit. Like other trusts designed for gifting, a GRAT is an irrevocable trust. As part of the trust agreement, the grantor establishes the amount that he or she will receive on at least an annual basis. In order to determine the gift tax on the transfer of the remainder interest, one takes the value of the assets transferred to the trust and subtracts the present value of the right to receive the annuity payments during the trust term. Through financial modeling, one can determine the optimum terms of the trust in order to establish the lowest gift tax possible (even zero under certain circumstances).

While there are a number of advantages and disadvantages to a GRAT, they remain an important technique for use in conjunction with the transfer of stock on a leveraged basis to the grantor's children and should be carefully considered. Consult with your attorney for more information about a GRAT.

Generation-Skipping Trusts. When the beneficiary of a transfer is in a generation which is two or more removed from the donor, the transfer is subject not only to a gift or estate tax, but is also subject to the generation-skipping transfer tax. This tax was aimed at the transfer of wealth which "skipped" a generation so that the Internal Revenue Service was unable to exact a tax on the transfer of wealth at each generation.

The administration of the generation-skipping tax is quite complex. When designing a generation-skipping trust, grandchildren or more remote descendants of the donor can be the sole beneficiaries of the trust, or the trust can be designed so the children of the donor can be beneficiaries during their lifetimes, followed by the grandchildren or more remote descendants. Substantial leverage can be gained by such multi-generational transfers of wealth. Check with your attorney to determine the current amount excluded from the application of the generation-skipping transfer tax, and whether this trust would benefit your individual circumstances.

Family Limited Partnerships Another common technique utilized for the transfer of assets is a family limited partnership ("FLP"). While FLPs can be used in conjunction with closely held stock, there are a number of unique problems that this scenario presents. For example, (S) corporation stock cannot be owned by an FLP. Therefore, caution is urged whenever a family partnership is contemplated in connection with the transfer of such business interests. More commonly, however, such an entity is used effectively for the transfer of real estate interests. Often, the real estate used to house the business is transferred to an FLP.

An FLP is one consisting of both general partnership interests and limited partnership interests. Typically, the general partnership interest is assigned a very small portion of the equity in the enterprise. Commonly, one or two percent of the value of the enterprise is assigned to the general partnership interests. The remainder of the equity interests is classified as limited partnership interests. The general partners are responsible for the management of the business enterprise, while the limited partners are given a limited or no voice in the management of the business. In addition, limited partners' interests are usually subject to various restrictions so that the interests cannot be transferred outside of a limited group, typically the family of the general partners, without first following a procedure established under the partnership agreement.

By transferring limited partnership interests to children or grandchildren of the donors or trusts for their benefit, one can move equity in a property, along with the income rights from such property at a substantially lower gift tax cost due to valuation discounts based on limited marketability and minority interests. As a result of these valuation discounts and overly aggressive use of family limited partnerships by some taxpayers, the IRS has raised challenges to this technique in many cases. Initially, the challenges related primarily to the valuation discounts. However, over the last few years, the IRS has had some success in challenging these arrangements on other grounds as well. Of principal concern to the estate planner have been issues involving the degree of control exercised by the general partners, who had transferred limited partnership interests to their descendants (or trusts for their descendants) and having personal use property as an asset of the partnership. While care must be taken in the design and management of the family limited partnership agreement, the technique can still produce some significant family and tax planning opportunities.

Your attorney will be critical to the proper development of an FLP and should be consulted on the details of managing it.

Valuations In order to establish the fair market value of any transfers, it is important to use a qualified appraiser to establish the value of the underlying assets as well as any applicable discounts that affect valuation. Typically, an appraiser must look at both the value of underlying assets and the applicable discounts in calculating the fair market value of the assets transferred. In some cases, it may be necessary to use different appraisers for this purpose. For example, in the context of a family limited partnership which holds real estate, it may be appropriate to have one appraiser establish the value of the real estate, which is contributed to the partnership, and a second appraiser who determines the appropriate discounts under the partnership agreement in order to calculate the value of limited partnership units. In this instance, the second appraiser will qualify the appraisal on the basis of accepting the value of the real estate as determined by the other appraiser.

Income Tax Basis   A taxpayer's income tax basis in an asset is the value originally paid for the asset plus qualified adjustments, such as the cost of improvements in the case of real estate. The adjusted income tax basis is important in determining a taxpayer's capital gain or loss on the disposition of the asset. When assets are transferred for no consideration by gift, the recipient takes the income tax basis that the donor would have had in the asset.

When making gifts of interests to family members or to charities, the income tax basis in the asset can be an important consideration, which must be factored into determining the recommended course of action.

Summary

Business owners also need to review their estate plan regularly with their attorney to keep it up to date due to changes in assets, heirs and your personal wishes. This includes Power of Attorney, healthcare directives and the naming of representatives and alternates.

At home one evening, take a look around your residence and ask yourself who would sort through everything if you were suddenly not there? Have you discussed your wishes with the person who would make estate decisions?

You may consider writing and sending a letter to the personal representative of your estate and his or her alternates outlining your wishes and detailing where vital estate information is filed. Sometimes personal representatives are included in discussions with your attorneys. A personal representative may be able to do a better job for your estate when given more information.

With the completion of your estate plan, this is an opportune time to organize your important paperwork and file it securely in a safe deposit box or a fireproof safe at home. Your attorney will provide you an organized folder of materials containing your will, trust documents and all other relevant documents outlining your affairs. Your financial planner will have given you some detailed paperwork, projections and plan documents regarding the financial decisions you have made during the process.

This is a good time to finish the job of detailing the other personal and financial information in your life that you deem important. Here is a sample list of other information that you may want to summarize and keep current to complete the process:

▶ Wills, trusts and other estate planning documents
▶ Current financial statement and financial planning documents
▶ General information such as date of birth, Social Security number, service number and other identifying numbers
▶ Birth certificates and military discharge paperwork
▶ List of advisors to be contacted in case of emergency
▶ Automobile titles
▶ List of bank accounts with name and telephone numbers of contacts
▶ Locations of safe-deposit boxes and their keys
▶ List of investment accounts with contact information
▶ List of insurance policies with contact information
▶ Detailed list of artwork, jewelry and other valuable possesions with appraisal or value information
▶ Legal documents describing ownership interests in any other businesses or real estate owned
▶ Locations of cemetery plots

It is much easier for you to organize your documents now than it will be for someone else to do it later.

Taking the time to completely organize your personal and financial information will prove to be valuable in keeping your affairs in order and will also serve as a road map for your spouse or personal representative later in life. You may want to let your attorney, spouse and children know where to look for the information, in case it is needed.

To begin your estate planning strategy, visit a trusts and estate attorney as soon as possible. Your attorney will help you develop your estate plan and play an important role in the eventual sale of your business.

Ethical Wills   Now that you've completed the necessary legal documents, this may also a good time to consider writing an ethical will. An ethical will is a non-legal, non-binding supplemental document that you prepare yourself. It is a tradition in which the writer passes on personal values, beliefs, blessings and advice to relatives and future generations. An ethical will may include memories, values, insights and special wisdom and experiences. An ethical will can further explain your wishes, and convey some family history and stories, among other information you may wish to include. For more information about ethical wills, you may want to read "Ethical Wills: Putting Your Values On Paper," by Barry K. Baines, M.D (www.ethicalwills.com). In it, Dr. Baines clearly explains the value of an ethical will and how to develop one. ■

6|The Business Profile

HOW DO YOU DEFINE your business? Before beginning the process of marketing the business, it is necessary to prepare a business profile. The profile explains your business to prospective buyers and includes information about the business, such as: general background and historical information, trade territory, number of customers, financial statements, equipment lists, inventory, real estate, employees, photos, marketing materials and other information that the buyer may find interesting.

You define what your business is; the M&A advisor communicates it to buyers

The purpose of the profile is to quantify what is being sold. Your M&A advisor will show your business as an opportunity.

The business profile will be sent to the prospective buyers after they have been qualified as seriously interested and financially able to afford a deal of the size and scope of your business. And prospective buyers will receive the business profile only after having signed a confidentiality agreement.

The business profile is not intended to take the place of the due diligence process, but rather to give the buyer enough information to decide whether or not to move forward. Information that is critical to the business—such as client lists, proprietary or confidential processes, tax returns, employee data and other information that might compromise the business—is not shared until a letter of intent or purchase agreement is signed.

The business profile is a chance for you to define your business and, in consultation with the M&A advisor, highlight the benefits and opportunities the buyer will realize by purchasing it. The business profile is a critical piece of the selling process. It will be the buyer's first contact with the business. The profile must entice the buyer, yet be accurate; exaggerating claims or understating opportunities easily turn away more buyers than they entice.

In order to entice and yet conform to confidentiality requirements, we prepare the profiles in two formats: The short form "teaser" and the long form sales presentation book.

The Short Form "Teaser"

The "teaser" is a short, anonymous one-page summary of your business and industry. Based on information contained in it, prospective buyers cannot determine what company is for sale, thus protecting your confidentiality.

The information is intended to invite interest in your company; it's just enough to whet their appetite, but not enough for them to figure out who you are. While every business is different, the short form typically contains:

- ▸ The type of business for sale and its history
- ▸ General location
- ▸ Real estate (owned or leased)
- ▸ Business activity summary
- ▸ Reason for selling (if appropriate)
- ▸ Gross and net income
- ▸ Other information as applicable

Sample copies of a short form teaser are shown on the next two pages.

A Sample Business Profile

Type of Business: Company is a fabricator of printed circuit boards supplied on a custom-build basis to the electronics industry. Located in the Midwest. Capabilities include:

— Prototype

— Quick turn

— Mid-volume production

— Multi-layer (up to 16 layers)

— Special materials: Teflon, polyamides, thermal materials, Teflon bonded to FR-4

— UL approved down to 3 mil lines/spaces

— 65% multi-layer; 35% double-sided

History: Sub-S corporation; started in 1975

Employees: 70 full-time; non-union

Customers: (by industry)

— Telecommunications	35%
— Medical	25%
— Consumer	20%
— Computers	20%

Quality:

— ISO 9002

— 80% of customers with company over 10 years

— Reject rates less than 2% from customers

Facilities: 25,000 sq.ft.

— Can be leased or purchased.

— Capacity to $15M

Reason for Sale: Owner desires retirement in 2 years

Financial Overview:

Year	Net Revenue	EBITDA
1997	$3.0M	$600K
1998	$3.5M	$900K
1999	$4.5M	$1.2M

A Sample Business Profile

Type of Business: Bindery company; related real estate

Location: Upper Midwest

Business Activity: Mechanical and adhesive binding

Real Estate: 25,000 sq.ft. industrial building on 5.0 acres; built in 1990

History: Company started in 1974; seller has owned for 14 years

Employees: 58 full-time, 2 part-time; non-union

Customers: Large commercial printers; paper manufacturers

Marketing: Referrals

Assets:

— Land and building appraised value of approximately $2M

— Business equipment, machinery, fixtures and furniture $800,000

Noteworthy: Company has documented processes, which are used for training and supervision enabling rapid transitions to new and different types of work.

Reason for Sale: Owner desires to pursue other interests.

Growth Area: Ideal buyer is strong in sales and marketing and/or could add production. Capacity in current facilities is $4M. Easy to expand facilities on existing property if buyer so desires.

Financial Overview:

Year	Sales	EBITDA
1998	$3.2M	$568K
1999	$2.7M	$445K
2000	$3.1M	$524K
2001	$3.3M	$595K

The "teaser" is attached to a letter of introduction and sent out to many prospective buyers; it is not unusual to target 250 to 300 prospective buyers. The letter, addressed to the president or the acquisition manager, is short and basically communicates that we have a profitable business for sale in the prospective buyer's industry.

Note that all communication regarding the letter and short form profile occurs through your M&A advisor. Customers, competitors and employees will not know that your business is for sale.

If a prospective buyer is interested in purchasing your business and you approve of the prospect, then your M&A advisor will proceed with signing confidentiality agreements and sending the prospective buyer the long form profile.

The Long Form Sales Presentation Book

The sales presentation book is the basis from which the "teaser" is derived. The sales presentation book is detailed and serves as a transition document that invites serious buyers to find out more about your business.

Typical buyers already know the industry and therefore can get a good sense of your business and its opportunities with some key information. That key information is contained in the sales presentation book. You could probably guess the key information simply by asking yourself this question: "Keeping in mind confidentiality issues, what information would I need to get a sense of my business's performance in my industry?"

The sales presentation book will be different for every business. Each business is unique and has different appealing aspects.

The presentation book typically includes the information on the following form.

BUSINESS PROFILE/SALES PRESENTATION INFORMATION

1. General Information Sheet
   a. Description of business
   b. History of business.
   c. Boundaries of trade area.
   d. Representative customer list (customer concentration information)
   e. Corporate structure and ownership information.
   f. Growth opportunities for business
   g. Capital equipment needs next three years
   h. Information on pending litigation, if any.

2. Last 3 years' financial statements – plus current year to date
   a. (Income & Expense, Balance Sheet). Other relevant data including:
   b. Information regarding nonrecurring income or expense items on operating statements.
   c. Breakdown of gross revenues including detail by product or service.
   d. Analysis of cost of goods sold. Information regarding recent trends as per centage of sales expenses.
   e. Projected income for next year
   f. Average accounts receivable balance.

3. Description of inventory and approximate dollar amount that will be part of the sale price. Sources of inventory.

4. Real estate ownership or lease, land and building dimensions, with square footage or storage capacities in tons, gallons or bushels, etc. Explanation of any environmental issues of concern. Maximum sales capacity at current locations.

5. List of furniture, fixtures, equipment, vehicles, leasehold improvements (depreciation schedule). Notation of any assets not included in the sale.

6. Information pertaining to management team and owners: salary, bonus, insurance and personal expenses. Resumes for key employees. Number of full- and part-time employees. Information regarding employee benefit and retirement plans. Organization chart. Incentive plans. Stock purchase plans. Phantom stock plans. ESOP.

7. Information supporting trademarks, copyrights, and proprietary registrations.

8. Contact information for advisors (accountant, attorney, financial planner, consul tants).

9. Any other information that would help define or sell the business.

Faelon Partners, Ltd.	763-231-4200	www.faelon.com

As you can see, the sales presentation book contains information that paints a very thorough picture of your business. Yet it does so in a simple format; the profile will be brief and direct. By the time the buyer has read through the profile, he or she should have a clear understanding of the business for sale.

The sales presentation book, then, sticks to the facts, allowing the buyer to come to independent conclusions about growth opportunities. That said, there are ways to make your business even more attractive.

Marketing Your Business

What makes your company special? Whatever it is, your M&A advisor should highlight it. This puts a "sizzle" on the business in order to get the highest price for it. What's the "sizzle"? The sizzle represents the opportunities your business offers a buyer. The sizzle compels buyers who are already interested to take a closer look.

Interested buyers want to see the opportunities to make money. Whatever is unique and compelling about the way your business turns a profit must be communicated to the buyer.

Prospective buyers are asking themselves: "Can I make money with this business?" Somebody will discover the opportunity in your business. That buyer will have the capabilities to increase profitability and grow the customer base. Whoever can most effectively increase profitability and grow the business will pay more than anyone else for it. Your M&A advisor's job is to find that buyer who can take the best advantage of the opportunity.

Just as important are opportunities to run the business efficiently. To this end, you are encouraged to explain clearly those expenses not directly related to producing and selling products.

One way to show this is by adjusting net income to add back any discretionary spending items, such as the owner's salary, owner's car expenses, and cell phone and home Internet accounts. This is to demonstrate the maximum cash flow available to the new owner to spend at his or her discretion.

We advise you to spend some time making certain that the owner's discretionary income is accurate because it is a very important number to a potential buyer.

Finally, geographic considerations may also play a role in marketing the business. Many sellers may already know who their primary buyers may be and where they're located. We market businesses locally, regionally or nationally based on the size of the business. You may have some possible buyers in mind; we will want to target them specifically.

That leads us to the questions: Who is going to buy your business and how do we contact them? In the next chapter, we answer those questions. ■

7 | Who's Going to Buy Your Business and How Do We Contact Them?

IF YOU HAD TO sell your business on your own, how would you approach the process? As a successful business owner, more than likely you would create a structure for the sale, market your business, qualify interested bidders and keep it all absolutely confidential. In other words, you would organize your selling effort. You should expect no less from your M&A advisor.

A structured sale means that your M&A advisor sells your business to another company within your industry niche by compiling a list of the businesses in the same industry that are larger than the one being sold.

This process is advantageous because it produces qualified buyers who have industry experience, are already operating larger, profitable companies and will know how to manage your business. Normally these industry buyers are referred to as "strategic buyers." They are strategic because they are buying within your industry in order to acquire market share, new customers, product lines or personnel needed to continue the growth of their own businesses.

In addition to the type of buyer, your M&A advisor targets a geographic area best suited for the size of the company being sold.

Generally speaking, the bigger the business is (in dollar terms), the bigger the geographic area in which to conduct a buyers search.

Finally, your M&A advisor must manage confidentiality between you and potential buyers.

Identifying Buyers

There are three types of business buyers. First are strategic buyers mentioned above. Second are private equity buyers, who are groups of professional investors with access to capital. Third are individual buyers. The M&A advisor will have information on all of the possible buyers and will be able to locate and contact them. Creating a targeted list of these buyers will be a joint effort between you and your advisor. Time must be spent on the process so that no qualified buyer is unintentionally omitted.

Strategic (Industry) Buyers Assuming that businesses in each industry want to grow, your M&A advisor can identify every business of a certain size in the industry by its SIC code. Every industry is part of the U.S. Government's Standard Industrial Classification Coding System (referred to as an SIC code), categorized by general business activity. There are thousands of SIC codes.

As businesses grow, it becomes increasingly difficult to continue a high rate of growth, so they turn to acquisitions in addition to organic growth. In short, most profitable companies are looking to acquire smaller businesses in their industry. They want to know what's available. Your M&A advisor can locate them by using their SIC codes.

For example, if your business has gross revenues of $10 million annually, your advisor will find those companies that are bigger than you with the same SIC code.

They are strategic buyers because they do the same thing in the same industry as you. They face the same problems you face. They compete for the same customers with the same or similar products. We'll assume they want to grow and that they'll be interested in acquiring other profitable businesses.

Here's an example of how finding strategic buyers can maximize the value of your business:

On one deal we found two separate strategic buyers that were in the process of buying up smaller businesses all over the United States. One was located on the East Coast and the other was in the Southeast. Our Midwestern firm was the biggest in the metropolitan area but a little under the size that each of the buying groups wanted. We were able to get both of them bidding on the company by supplying the demographic data on the area to convince the buyers that the trade area of the seller was large enough to facilitate significant growth. In this case a long-standing profitable business wasn't enough until we showed that it had great potential to continue its rapid growth.

As a seller, you probably already know who the likely buyers of your business may be; in fact, the best buyer might be your toughest competitor, with whom you don't want to have direct contact (this is a confidentiality issue and will be discussed later in this chapter). Contacting competitors about buying your business is an ideal situation for an M&A advisor who can confidentially determine their level of interest in buying a sound, profitable business.

The following story demonstrates how strategic marketing can locate the most qualified buyer for your business.

We had a business to sell in a rural Midwestern town that was family owned and operated, with just under $2 million in revenue. The owner was making a very good living. The business was difficult to market because it did not generate enough income to attract the larger national buyers. This was interesting because the seller was retirement age and was serious about selling but wanted to find someone with industry knowledge to buy it.

We compiled a list of businesses in the industry that were the same size or larger from the seven closest states. The list consisted of about 350 businesses. The marketing program resulted in many inquiries, which were assessed and eventually reduced to four qualified buyer groups. Each buyer group owned a business of similar size. Oddly enough, each buyer group had too many family members trying to live off of those businesses. The groups' members included: a father and son; two brothers; four brothers; and two brothers from out of state.

In the end one of the brother-groups cut a deal to buy out one brother and allow him to use the proceeds to move to the seller's town and buy the business. This was a classic example of how strategic marketing can locate experienced and financially qualified buyers.

Private Equity Buyers   The second major group of possible buyers is the private equity groups. Many thousands of independent investment groups in the United States raise capital to invest in private businesses, search for and purchase portfolio companies, manage and grow them for a period of years and then sell when they have reached an appropriate size to realize their targeted return on investment. These groups are generally stratified by size of investment and also by the size of portfolio companies owned, on whose behalf they make acquisitions to achieve growth objectives.

We work to find the buyer who can afford to pay more for your company than any other buyer

A classic example of an interested equity buyer would involve a group that already owns one or more (portfolio) companies in a particular industry. While a private equity buyer typically wants to purchase larger businesses, a smaller one may be purchased in order to increase the size of the portfolio business. Ultimately the goal will be to take the portfolio company to the market and sell it once it reaches a predetermined size and profitability.

In short, your M&A advisor must know who's looking to buy in each industry. He or she should maintain a comprehensive list of equity buyers compiled over time and based on a history of relationships with those buyers.

Independent (Individual) Buyer   The third kind of buyer is an individual or family. This is the most time-consuming group to deal with because it is so diverse. Buyers come with a full range of financial requirements and strategies. Their diverse nature makes them difficult to categorize and target as a group. Sometimes a family looks to buy in order to diversify its holdings. Executives between jobs might decide to buy and run a company instead of returning to corporate America.

Who could maximize the profits from my revenue streams?

Your M&A advisor should have accumulated and maintained a list of independent buyers who want to purchase businesses. It is a dynamic list that is always in a state of change.

By constantly keeping track of independent buyers we were able to sell a very profitable business to a family buyer. In this case the family had sold a multimillion-dollar business and was looking for some smaller businesses to purchase for younger family members to operate. Since the younger family member did not have expertise in the business, we were able to negotiate for the sellers to stay on with the company for a period of 3 years to train in the new buyer, and in exchange the sellers got a great price and an attractive earn-out bonus for helping run the business during a long transition period.

Qualifying a Buyer

Once your M&A advisor has compiled a list of targeted buyers, he or she will send out a short "teaser" letter (the short form of the business profile) in order to attract buyers. Some of them will call in for more information. Your advisor will begin qualifying them at that moment. He or she will find out what companies are interested, how long the companies have been in business, company revenues and how many people each one employs. In addition, he or she will locate Web sites and will note anything else of interest to help determine the viability of the interested parties. Your advisor should try to identify the buyers that are best positioned to make the most profit from your business' revenue stream(s).

A business in your industry — whether local, national or international — may be able to buy the raw materials cheaper, might have better lines of distribution or a larger sales team that can sell a higher volume of product.

Your M&A advisor is looking for qualified buyers that have the time, money and expertise to buy and operate your business profitably. These buyers can afford to pay more money for your business and have a better probability of success at running your business profitably than do other buyers.

Here's an example:

"Don't overlook your suppliers!"

In one sale, we were able to sell a business at a price that was 40 percent more than the next nearest offer because we sold it to the supplier. Since the supplier could obtain significantly higher margins due to the fact that it had a lower cost of goods sold than anyone else and it could pick up some market share within its territory, it was able to pay more. This came down to the buyer having two profit margins (one wholesale and one retail) to benefit from within the gross sales of the seller.

You and the M&A advisor must spend some time analyzing who the best-qualified buyers for the business might be. It is important for the your advisor to completely understand your business in order to compile a list of the businesses in your industry and determine the best way to contact them.

If the potential buyers want to move forward, your M&A advisor provides you with qualifying information. After you've had time to review the qualifying information, you grant (or deny) permission to pursue more detailed contact with the prospective buyers. Typically, "more detail" translates into providing the buyer with the long form sales presentation book after confidentiality issues are resolved.

Seller Confidentiality Issues

Before any prospective buyer is allowed to see the long form sales presentation book, a confidentiality agreement must be signed. Confidentiality is essential to your financial security. Confidentiality cannot be overstated; nor can it be underemphasized to prospective buyers.

Your M&A advisor will require that all contacts go through him or her. The buyer is forbidden to contact the company, employees of the company, customers of the company and any person or any business associated with the company.

Signatories to confidentiality agreements are usually business owners and/or high-level managers. They understand confidentiality issues and respect them; they wouldn't want to lose employees or customers either. They understand that confidentiality is a moral and legal obligation.

Once we are convinced that the interested party is sincere about buying the business and maintaining confidentiality, and we have the seller's permission, we send a confidentiality agreement for the buyer to sign. A sample agreement follows.

Sample Confidentiality Agreement

This Agreement, made and entered into this _____ day of _____ 20___, by and between _____; (Seller) and _____; (Buyer).

WITNESSETH:

WHEREAS, Buyer desires to review the business operations, assets and financial documents of Seller in order to assist Buyer in deciding whether or not to enter into purchase negotiations with Seller; and

WHEREAS, Buyer is currently engaged in_____ which business is very similar to a portion of Seller's business; and

WHEREAS, Seller and Buyer mutually acknowledge and agree that any such disclosure would constitute unfair competition; and

WHEREAS, any damages occasioned by such disclosure or business expansion would be difficult to estimate or ascertain,

NOW, THEREFORE, in consideration of the above and the mutual covenants and agreements contained herein, the parties hereto agree as follows:

Seller shall make available to Buyer such books, records and files as it may reasonably request to facilitate its review of Seller's assets and financial condition.

All such information provided to Buyer by Seller, as well as any information obtained by Buyer as a direct or indirect result of information provided by Seller, shall remain confidential and shall not be disclosed by Buyer to any third party not similarly agreeing to hold such information in confidence. Prior to any such disclosure to a third party, Buyer shall obtain the approval of Seller and shall obtain from such third party a written confidentiality agreement. While we consider the enclosed information to be reliable, FAELON has not verified it and makes no guarantee, warranty or representation about it.

In the event that the business of Seller is not ultimately purchased by Buyer, Buyer agrees that any and all information furnished by Seller to Buyer shall be returned within ten (10) days of the termination of the parties' negotiations, together with all copies thereof, and along with all notes and other records or information relating to Seller's business which were provided by Seller or otherwise obtained by Buyer. Buyer agrees that it shall not act upon, utilize or disseminate any information received or obtained by Buyer arising out of Buyer's investigation of Seller's assets or financial condition. Said prohibition on Buyer's utilization of Seller's confidential information shall preclude Buyer from soliciting Seller's employees and/or customers. Therefore, Buyer hereby agrees that, for a period of one (1) year following the conclusive termination of negotiations between the parties, it shall not unfairly compete with Seller by soliciting Seller's employees and/or customers.

Buyer agrees that it will disclose such information to its officers, directors,employees and agents only on a "need to know" basis.

Seller and Buyer agree that, because of the difficulty involved in estimating damages, and because of potential for irreparable harm which may result to Seller from Buyer's disclosure of Seller's confidential information or from Buyer's solicitation of Seller's employees and/or customers, this Agreement shall be enforceable by injunction or other equitable relief, as well as by suit for damages (or both if allowed under applicable law).

Buyer warrants and represents that it is authorized to execute this Agreement and that it shall use its best efforts to prevent the dissemination of any of Seller's confidential information by Buyer's directors, officers, employees or agents.

Seller agrees to be bound by the same terms and conditions provided herein regarding any information learned about Buyer's business, employees and customers during the process of negotiating for the sale of Seller's business to Buyer.

The parties hereto mutually acknowledge and agree that this Agreement shall be governed by and interpreted under the laws of the State of Minnesota, and the exclusive jurisdiction and venue for any dispute arising from or related to this Agreement shall be the State Circuit Court.

If any part of this Agreement is later determined to be void or otherwise unenforceable, this shall not affect the validity and enforceability of the remainder of this agreement and, further, the Court shall be authorized and empowered to enforce the invalidated provision(s) to the maximum extent permitted by law.

Buyer hereby acknowledges that the Business and/or Property referred to herein is subject to a listing agreement between Seller and Faelon; was presented to Buyer by Faelon; Faelon is acting exclusively as the Seller's broker in this transaction, and that Buyer has received a copy of this Confidentiality Agreement as of the date hereof.

Due to the confidential nature of this listing, please make all contacts through FAELON and under no circumstances contact the Seller directly or Seller's employees or clients!

IN WITNESS THEREOF, the parties hereto have executed this Agreement as of the day and year first above written.

Buyer

By _____

Once a signed confidentiality agreement is in hand, we can send out the sales presentation book.

The risks to your business are too great to allow confidentiality to be compromised in any way. An M&A advisor must be unconditionally confidential about the sale of your business. Confidentiality protects you, your employees and your customers.

An M&A advisor will constantly remind buyers that discussions and knowledge of the pending sale of your company are private and confidential.

The following scenario is how one sale rolled out:

- ▸ The M&A advisor sent out 280 "teasers" with a short letter of introduction.
- ▸ From those 280 mailings, the M&A advisor received 40 inquiries from interested parties.
- ▸ Of those 40 inquiries, the advisor qualified the buyers and received the seller's permission to send out 15 sales presentation books.
- ▸ Nine firms responded with an indication of value, the amount they'd pay for the business.
- ▸ Of those nine firms, the advisor ended up with two serious buyers.
- ▸ The deal was closed shortly after negotiating the sale with the best buyer for the business.

As the deal closes, the M&A advisor should go back to the firms who received the sales presentation books and ask to have them returned. Also he or she should remind them of the confidentiality agreement and ask them not to talk about the sale, or contact the company, its employees or customers.

The confidentiality process is critical to protect the value of your business as well as your financial future and all the hard work you've put into building the business. The M&A advisor will manage this critical part of the selling process for you.

For those sellers who are less concerned about the confidentiality issues as it relates to the marketing plan we have outlined in this book, other venues will be available to market your business for sale. These include advertisements in the Wall Street Journal and local newspapers, business publications, trade magazines and Internet resources.

It will be important for you and your M&A advisor to decide on the degree of confidentiality required to implement your marketing plan at the beginning of the process. ∎

8| Your Accountant

THIS CHAPTER WAS WRITTEN with generous contributions of time and expertise by Jeffrey W. Starbird.

> *Jeffrey W. Starbird, CPA, JD, is a partner in the accounting firm of Lurie, Besikof, Lapidus & Company, LLP. He holds undergraduate degrees in Accounting and Economics from St. John's University in Collegeville, Minnesota. Mr. Starbird graduated from William Mitchell College of Law and, in 1980, entered the Minnesota Bar. He is a frequent lecturer on a multitude of complex tax issues. He is a member of the American Institute of Certified Public Accountants, the Minnesota Society of CPAs, the American Bar Association and the American Association of Attorney-Certified Public Accountants, Inc. His areas of expertise include assisting clients in a variety of tax examination matters, business and individual income taxation and estate planning.*

In addition to discussing accounting and tax strategy, accountants help business owners prepare for and facilitate the sale of their businesses. The accountant should be closely involved in developing your goals as they relate to the sale of your business. Prior to the sale and during the selling process, the accountant will keep an overall view of the financial and tax implications of the sale. He or she will keep their eyes on the big picture because every seller — you included — will experience a great deal of emotion when selling your business and may not be able to think in terms of the big picture as objectively as your accountant can.

Selecting an Accountant

Because the accountant's role in the sale of your business is so critical, it is important to choose an experienced professional. Experience in M&A is a must for your accountant to be the effective advisor you need. Ask your accountant about his or her M&A transactions experience. Be aware that sometimes it may not be the particular accountant that you have worked with over the years who has the experience. It may be another accountant in that office with the experience that you seek. If necessary, your M&A advisor can tactfully approach the topic with your accountant. If it turns out that your accountant is inexperienced in mergers and acquisitions, then you should ask for an M&A referral or ask your accountant to team up with a more experienced accountant.

Accountants involved in a business transaction should be certified public accountants (CPA). Most will be members of the American Institute of Certified Public Accountants (AICPA) and, as such, must follow strict rules and reporting standards set forth by the AICPA. Your CPA must be experienced with whatever accounting method is used by your business, whether you use the cash basis, income tax basis, or standards set forth by Generally Accepted Accounting Principles (GAAP).

It is important to use a CPA or accounting firm with the vision and ability to bring two sides together in a tax-efficient manner that coincides with your goals. You need a CPA who is experienced in dealing with the nuances of the tax law.

The Accountant's Role in the Selling Process

The CPA has a unique position in the process of selling your business. Your CPA will assist the M&A advisor in crafting a structure and seeking middle ground in a win-win scenario for you and the buyer. That gives the CPA considerable flexibility to make unilateral suggestions. In the event problems arise, the CPA might be able to suggest compromises that both parties may agree to. This underscores the true role of the CPA: to help you maximize your return upon the sale of your business and minimize income taxes on the transaction.

To that end, the CPA performs several very important functions in the selling process.

Accounting, Financial Statements and Taxes The CPA prepares all of the financial statements; chances are he or she has done this task for you for some time. The clearer and more precise your financial and tax documents are prepared for the buyer's review, the faster the review process will move and the more likely the buyer will develop trust in you. One example of "clearer and more precise" would be the footnotes in your financial statements. Footnotes must be comprehensive, clear and readable for the buyer and his or her CPA.

Conversely, if the financial documents are incomplete, inaccurate or difficult to understand, the buyer is more likely to question them and other parts of your business.

Pricing Your Business The M&A advisor and the CPA also help you set a selling price for your business. Pricing is one of the challenges of selling a business and it takes an experienced CPA to help get the job done in an accurate manner.

When your CPA presents you with a price, a good question to ask is this: "How can a buyer buy my business at the price you're suggesting and have it be a good investment for that person?"

If the accountant can reasonably support an assessment, then you probably have a good target price. With that, you and your

M&A advisor can set an asking price that gives some room for negotiations.

M&A Experience   As noted earlier, experience in mergers and acquisitions is important. Every deal has surprises. CPAs experienced in mergers and acquisitions know how to respond to those surprises. This holds true for your M&A advisor as well. An experienced advisor can guide the selling process through those inevitable obstacles and surprises and bring the process to a successful closure.

Selling your business can be hampered by severe tax consequences. An experienced accountant can help you understand very complicated rules and assist you in structuring the sale. Here's an example of a potential tax trap. Selling business assets from as S corporation typically results in personal tax to the owner. However, if within the last 10 years a company was a C corporation, an additional corporate level tax could be due. This double taxation (or "built-in-gains" tax) could be significant enough to postpone the deal until the 10-year period expires. Another way to avoid the tax would be to sell stock versus assets. Many business owners are unaware of this tax and would be in for an unwelcome surprise when they receive their tax returns.

Other more complex surprises are sure to pop up during the selling process. Every deal has your side and the buyer's side; experience and resourcefulness are required to find the middle ground, get you the best price and allow the buyer every opportunity to succeed.

Business Organization

The CPA brings knowledge of how your business is organized and how it has been taxed in the past. Accounting and taxation laws may apply differently to your business depending on how it is organized.

Typically, a business' organization will be defined as one of the following:

- Regular (C) corporation
- Pass-through (S) corporation
- Limited liability company (LLC) or partnership (LLP)
- Sole-proprietor or partnership

Your business's organization will influence the structure of the sale and is therefore a starting point in developing your sale position.

Tax Structure of the Sale

The CPA will help you decide how to structure the deal. At issue is taxation and cash flow. The CPA structures the deal so that it conforms to the tax laws and accounting ethics and at the same time meets your cash flow requirements and those of the buyer. The goal is to minimize the tax ramifications to you while maximizing cash flow.

Stock Sales, Asset Sales and Their Tax Ramifications There are generally two choices on the structure of the sale of a business: a stock sale and an asset sale. In a stock sale, you sell the history and outright ownership of the business, both assets and liabilities. In an asset sale, you sell only the assets, including customer lists and other profit supporting aspects of the business and keep most liability (unless negotiated otherwise) and keep the corporate shell.

Due to capital gains tax rates generally being lower than ordinary tax rates, sellers typically prefer stock sales.

Under a stock sale structure, an accountant can readily determine the taxes payable as a result of the sale. This is important because it can affect how much tax the seller pays during the year of the sale.

For example:

Sellers should be aware of a potentially serious trap when the buyer offers a mixture of cash and buyer's stock. In one situation, a seller negotiated a $10,000,000 deal where *he would receive $6,500,000 in cash and $3,500,000 worth of the acquiring company's stock. The seller knew he would have to pay tax on the cash, but thought the tax on the stock would be delayed until he actually sold it. Luckily, he ran the transaction by his accountant. He was told that the IRS would tax the fair market value of the stock because the percentage of cash was too high to allow the stock portion of the purchase price to be tax-deferred. The IRS has indicated it will not question up to 50 percent cash and the rest stock, but would tax the entire amount if the percentage of cash were higher than 50 percent. If this deal had closed as negotiated, the seller would have used his cash to pay tax on the cash received and the stock received.*

So the M&A advisor and the accountant would have to determine if there was a way to defer the tax until the remaining stock is sold and the proceeds are received. An experienced team might be able to accomplish this.

The buyer will have different ideas about how to structure the deal. The buyer usually doesn't want a stock purchase, primarily because of the potential legal liability issues. The buyer will want to purchase certain assets, assume certain liabilities and recognize the fair market value of furniture, fixtures and equipment to increase future depreciation expense. However, that could increase the amount of money you receive subject to ordinary income tax, which can be significantly higher than capital gains tax. That means less money for you after taxes.

An astute M&A advisor will want to understand the financial results of the structure and work with your CPA to minimize the tax consequences. And, your broker should help you ask all of the appropriate questions of your CPA to ensure your understanding of the outcome of the transaction.

Your CPA and M&A attorney will play critical roles in determining the best structure to serve your interests. Because the buyer has subjective interests in how the deal is structured, a great deal of negotiation and thoughtfulness may be called for.

Much negotiation and resourcefulness may be necessary at this point in the selling process. The CPA is busy assessing financial issues that affect you, while the M&A attorney is determining the appropriate allocations and the best legal language to use to describe the deal. Your CPA will want to review the documents to ensure that they correctly reflect the desired tax implications as planned. With your approval, the CPA and the attorney advise the M&A advisor on how to negotiate the deal in a way that benefits you and yet addresses the needs and concerns of the buyer.

Deals that fall apart usually do so at this point in the process. Sometimes the buyer and seller get stuck and don't know where to go. Your CPA and M&A advisor can usually find ways to move the deal forward and still meet the needs of each side.

However the sale is structured, the M&A advisor and CPA work together so that you walk away with the most money from the sale of your business.

Allocating the Purchase Price

Allocating the purchase price tends to be somewhat anticlimactic but still important. In fact, often the transaction attorneys (See Chapter Nine) handle the details of the allocations along with the purchase agreement. Both the seller and the buyer generally must report the allocation in their business income tax return.

There are many ways to allocate, or account for, the price the buyer is willing to pay you for your business. We've already discussed the tax ramifications of the structure of the deal; how the purchase price is allocated may also affect how much tax you pay. Another consideration is lifestyle, as discussed in Chapter Four: The Personal Financial Planner. For example, do you expect the business to continue to pay you and your family benefits such as health insurance? If so, then benefits would be accounted for in the allocation of the purchase price.

As M&A advisors we try to ensure that all the questions have been asked on your behalf

When talking about allocating the purchase price, the transaction attorney and the CPA will have significant input; the M&A advisor will make sure the team talks about the various allocations and their effects on you. By raising the questions, he or she is attempting to provide you with the greatest number of options available to meet your financial, tax and lifestyle choices.

Keep in mind that each tax consequence subtracts from the overall net cash received from the sale of your business. Knowing the tax consequences of the various allocations prior to allocating the purchase price is critical to maximizing the amount of money you net from the sale.

Some of the purchase price may be allocated to an "earnout." An earnout is a payment structure that is contingent on the continued performance and future profitability of the business. This form of payment gives the buyer some confidence that the business will not disintegrate once you are out of the picture. While an earnout means you stay involved with the business to help hold the customer base together, it may help you increase the potential to realize more money from the sale while helping to ensure the buyer of future success.

Benefits — such as health insurance, use of a car, and travel expenses, among many others — may receive allocations from the purchase price. Whatever the allocation, the M&A advisor and CPA will work to structure the deal in a way that is best for you and agreeable to the buyer.

In general, everything about the company — including intangible assets such as goodwill, copyrights and trademarks — will be allocated a portion of the purchase price. You, your CPA and your M&A advisor will work to decide which tax consequences of those allocations are acceptable to you and which are not. Based on those decisions, your team will try to find solutions acceptable to both you and the buyer.

Example of Selling Assets Versus Stock

	Asset Sale	Stock Sale
Sale Price	10,000,000	5,863,000
Basis of Corporate Assets	0	0
Gain at Corporate Level	10,000,000	5,863,000
Corporate Tax (State: 9.8%)	(980,000)	0
Gain Taxable for Federal Tax Purposes	9,020,000	0
Corporate Tax (Federal: 35%)	(3,157,000)	0
Proceeds to Shareholder (Sale Price Less Corporate Taxes)	5,863,000	5,863,000
Shareholder's Basis in Stock	1,000	1,000
Cash to Shareholder	5,862,000	5,862,000
Individual Tax (State: 8%)	(468,960)	(468,960)
Gain Taxable for Federal Tax Purposes	5,393,040	5,393,040
Individual Tax (Federal: 15%)	(808,956)	(808,956)
Net Cash	4,584,084	4,584,084

Assumptions

▶ Company is taxed as a regular Minnesota C Corporation
▶ Seller has owned the business for many years and has fully depreciated the company's assets
▶ Seller's original investment was $1,000 for 100% of the common stock

The tax on sale of S corporation stock is identical to C corporation stock. The big advantage of an S corporation is when only the assets are sold. Using this example, S corporation assets are sold with the same lower tax of a stock sale, avoiding the double tax of the C corporation asset sale. The primary exception to this result is when assets are sold in a business that was originally a C corporation and elected to S status within 10 years.

The earlier you get your CPA involved in the process of selling your business, the sooner you can define the tax structure and its benefits and the smoother the selling process will be. ■

9 | The Transaction Attorney

THIS CHAPTER WAS WRITTEN with generous contributions of time and expertise by Timothy R. Duncan.

> *Timothy R. Duncan is a partner with the law firm of Coleman, Hull & van Vliet, PLLP, in Minneapolis, Minnesota. He represents small to mid-range businesses with respect to all aspects of their commercial legal needs, including entity formation, shareholder/corporate issues, contracts, employment and mergers and acquisitions.*

While the transaction attorney's role in a business sale may typically be perceived as preparing and reviewing transaction documents, the attorney should be involved in all three aspects of a business sale: (1) preparing the business for sale; (2) negotiating and documenting the transaction; and (3) closing the transaction and addressing post-closing matters.

The transaction attorney's involvement in the preparation of a business sale should be hand-in-hand with the business owner, as well as the owner's businesses professionals, including an M&A advisor, financial planner, trusts and estate attorney, and CPA. The extent of legal involvement in preparing a business for sale often is dependent upon the extent the business owner has kept its legal house in order prior to the transaction. The preparation process from a legal perspective primarily entails two areas, the first being general business legal issues, and the second structuring both the business for sale and the transaction itself.

Preparation: General Business Legal Issues

Corporate Issues   The business corporate records and documents should be reviewed and updated to ensure proper memorialization of corporate ownership, board positions, officers and any other significant corporate events that have occurred prior to the anticipated business sale. All share or equity ownership issues should be clarified. All ownership interests need to be properly memorialized, and any potential corporate sales restrictions, buy/sell agreements or rights of first refusal should be clarified to ensure that there is no ownership dispute and there are no restrictions or prohibitions on the proposed transaction. Once clarified, the ownership and governing board of the selling entity will have to properly authorize the transaction.

Structure   The business to be sold should be clearly identified (assets in the case of an asset sale and equity in the case of a stock or membership interest sale). All title and interest to either the assets or the ownership equity must be clarified and confirmed to be free and clear of any third-party claims to title, liens or other encumbrances. All intellectual property should be confirmed as properly registered with the pertinent government offices.

Real Estate Issues   Business real estate should be addressed early in the sale process. If the business owns both the operating business and the property in one entity, an owner that does not wish to sell the property with the business should consider transferring the property to a separate legal entity or excluding the property from the sale being careful not to accidentally trigger a taxable event. The owner should also have the property title examined to determine that the title is clear, and if not, start the process of clearing title. If the property is sold with the business, the owner should firm up any tenant leases, inspect the property condition, and remedy any defects or problems. If the property is leased, most leases require the landlord's prior written consent before it is assigned to a buyer. The landlord will review and approve/decline the buyer as a new tenant, while attempting to hold the seller liable under terms of the original lease. The transaction attorney should assist in notifying the landlord, obtaining the necessary consents, and attempting to convince the landlord to negotiate a new direct lease with the buyer and terminate the seller's lease entirely to preclude any future seller liability.

Litigation and Claims   If possible, any pending litigation, disputes, warranty claims or other proceedings should be resolved to ensure there are no third-party claims against title or assets of the business, and to avoid any insecurity on the part of potential buyers.

Contractural Issues   Many business contracts provide that the other contracting party has the right to cancel a contract or require consent to assignment of the contract in the event a business is sold. Since many business contracts are of fundamental importance to a potential buyer, it is necessary to review all contracts for these restrictions, determine if consents are required, and attempt to obtain consents or confirm continuation of the contracts following a transaction. Further, if the business has ongoing relationships which are not memorialized by a contract, attempts should be made to formalize the contractual relationship.

Employment Matters   Numerous employment issues arise with respect to the sale of a business which will require legal review, including determination of whether there are existing employment contracts that bind the business following the sale, the existence of employee-employment, confidentiality and non-competition provisions, the existence of any union contracts or federal or state law requiring notices and registration of any business sale, the transfer and closing out of employment benefit plans, and a business owner's desire to provide for the continued employment and opportunities of its existing valued employees.

Financial and Insurance Matters   Most business owners have relationships with financial institutions which have loaned funds pursuant to notes, security agreements and guarantees, all of which place liens and restrictions on the transfer and sale of business assets. These financial issues have to be addressed in preparation for the transaction. Similarly, the business owner not only has to consider the cancellation of existing commercial insurance, but whether or not to purchase insurance to provide liability protection following the sale, often referred to as "tail" insurance coverage.

Preparation: Pre-Sale Structural Considerations

Once the general business legal preparations are completed, the business owner must determine how the transaction will be structured, as the structure will have significant tax, liability and operational impact on all parties concerned. Transactions are typically structured as either the sale of the company's assets or the company's equity (stock, membership interest or partnership interest). Buyers usually prefer purchases through separately formed acquisition entities to minimize successor liability. The M&A advisor will help business owners consult with their accountant and transaction attorney to determine the best structure of the transaction.

Negotiating and Documenting the Transaction

Documenting and completing the transaction typically starts with negotiating the transactional representative's contracts, completing confidentiality agreements, preparing a letter of intent, outlining the transaction and then negotiating and completing the underlying transaction documents.

Confidentiality Agreement   Given the sensitive nature of the transaction and the need to exchange highly confidential information regarding the business, an initial document completed by the transaction attorney is a confidentiality agreement. The confidentiality agreement will establish virtually all the information disclosed by the selling business as confidential, prohibit the disclosure of such information, and require the return or destruction of all confidential information if the transaction is not completed. Confidentiality agreements usually include terms which protect the proprietary rights of the selling party in its products as well as terms restricting competition with the selling company's customers, employees or contractors if the deal falls through.

Letter of Intent   Once the business has been marketed and a prospective buyer indicates an interest in purchasing the business, the transaction attorney assists in the negotiation of a preliminary document outlining the general terms of the transaction. This written understanding may be in the form of a letter of intent, memorandum of understanding or term sheet. The written document, signed by both parties, is important to outline the terms of the transaction and to provide proof of the parties' commitment to proceed with the negotiations and document the transaction. The letter of intent then forms the framework for the completion of more formal transaction documents. As a result, it is important for the seller to retain legal counsel prior to signing the letter of intent to protect the seller's legal interestes and encure the transaction is properly structured.

Typical letter of intent deal points include the following:

▸ The identity of the selling and purchasing parties
▸ A description of what is purchased (i.e., what assets or equiy)
▸ The purchase price and payment terms
▸ If financed, the terms of any security pledged by the purchaser
▸ A description of the transaction documents to be negotiated and signed
▸ Conditions and contingencies for closing
▸ A drop-dead closing date and due diligence period
▸ Exclusivity or "no shop" terms
▸ Confidentiality terms
▸ Terms outlining what letter of intent terms, if any, are binding
▸ Earnest money or buy-back provisions

While a letter of intent is not usually legally binding as a whole, certain provisions such as confidentiality, exclusivity or earnest money provisions often are deemed binding. To further ensure the seriousness of a buyer's interest, the seller may demand earnest money terms. However, earnest money and other side agreements will be resisted by a purchaser or subject to significant contingency language permitting the purchaser to back out of the deal if certain financing or other due diligence contingencies are not satisfied.

Due Diligence   Once the letter of intent is executed, and while the parties negotiate the more definitive terms of the transaction documents, the buyer conducts its due diligence. The role of the transaction attorney in the due diligence process is somewhat limited. However, the transaction attorney will assist the seller in the preparation and disclosure of corporate and legal documentation, addressing any questions regarding pending litigation or contractual issues, and otherwise ensure the confidentiality of information disclosed during the due diligence process.

Purchase Agreement   Upon completion of the letter of intent, the next step is the negotiation and completion of the purchase agreement, which memorializes the terms and conditions of the transaction. Since each transaction is unique, the terms and conditions of purchase agreements vary as well.

Based upon the terms agreed upon in the letter of intent, the buyer's counsel usually prepares the purchase agreement and forwards the draft document to the seller and the seller's transaction attorney for review and comments. While the basic transaction terms have been agreed upon, the terms of the purchase agreement may require significant ongoing negotiation. The attorney-as-counselor role may come into play at this point as the buyer and seller engage an intense negotiation process. Typical purchase agreement terms are as follows:

Identity of the Parties   All parties who have rights under the transaction should be identified in the purchase agreement.

Identification of the Assets In an asset purchase, the parties will want to properly list all assets purchased, whereas a stock purchase will identify the proportions and equity purchased. Assets purchased do not simply include hard assets such as furniture, fixtures and equipment, but also intangible assets such as intellectual property (trademarks, trade names, and patents), contractual relationships, customer lists/relationships and other intangibles. The agreement should specifically list what liabilities, including contractual obligations, if any, are to be assumed by the purchaser. The agreement should also list what assets the seller wishes to exclude from the transaction.

Purchase Price   There are several different methods to establish the purchase price for the business. The purchase price may be a firm purchase price, a variable purchase price or earnout based upon certain negotiated formulaic or sales terms, or a contingent purchase price wherein the purchase price is adjusted based upon the computation of post-closing receivables and costs. The agreement also should provide for an allocation of the purchase price among the assets as required by the Internal Revenue Code, which will have to be set out in a form filed with the IRS. The seller should consult with his or her CPA as the tax ramifications of the allocation of the purchase price can be significant.

Payment Terms   When the purchase price is not for an agreed sum paid at closing, the agreement must set forth definitive payment terms. Installment payment terms should be further memorialized by a promissory note and subject to security. Some agreements provide for a hold-back or escrow of funds to be released upon the occurrence of certain triggering events or the passage of time. Contingent or earnout payments further must be identified, with the parties agreeing not only on the calculation of the earnout or contingent payments, but the timing and amount of the payments.

Representations and Warranties   A major issue in most purchase agreements is the seller's representations and warranties section. The buyer justifiably desires numerous representations and warranties from the seller outlining the condition of the business being sold because of the natural imbalance of knowledge between the parties regarding the status of the business. The representations and warranties provide the buyer a measure of assurance that the condition of the business is sound or as promised by the seller. A seller will desire to limit the representations and warranties to a reasonable extent to limit post-closing libability.

Likewise, the buyer will provide representations and warranties for the seller. These usually are minimal, and limited to assurances that the buyer is properly organized, has authority to complete the transaction, is not subject to any litigation, and has received all the necessary consents to complete the transaction.

Covenants and Obligations   Additional covenants and obligations are often written into the purchase agreement. If a closing is set for a date after the intitial signing of a purchase agreement, these covenants dictate what happens in the time period between signing the purchase agreement and the actual closing, and pertain to issues such as operating the business in a normal manner. They may also include certain post-closing agreements, such as an agreement not to compete for a certain length of time.

Non-Competition and Confidentiality   The purchase agreement may contain a provision which the parties agree to keep not only the terms of the transaction confidential, but also not to disclose any confidential or proprietary information with respect to the purchased business. Equally important to the purchasing entity are non-competition terms, which may be negotiated to the buyer and seller's satisfaction and memorialized in a separate agreement.

Liability Limitations and Indemnity   Most purchase agreements contain provisions in which the parties' representations and warranties will survive for a set number of years following the closing. The seller will want to limit this timeframe and the corresponding liability. Conversely, the buyer will wish to seek protection from the seller's representations and warranties as long as possible. Both parties should agree to indemnification provisions in which the seller indemnifies the buyer from any material breaches of the purchase agreement as well as the operation of the business prior to the closing date, while the buyer indemnifies the seller for any breaches of the purchase agreement and operation of the business following the closing date.

Miscellaneous Terms   All purchase agreements include several miscellaneous provisions at the end of the document. These miscellaneous terms may set out the applicable state law and jurisdiction, establish dispute resolution procedures, restrict assignment rights, and outline notice terms.

Related Purchase Documents   The purchase agreement will include and reference additional documents in the transaction. These documents may include, but are not limited to: documents related tansfer of title to the assets, financing, security for payment, assumed contracts, key employees, non-competition, and more.

Closing and Post-Closing Matters

Provided the purchase documentation is properly negotiated and completed, the transaction closing may be rather uneventful. As stated, most business sales are simultaneous closings, meaning the purchase documentation is negotiated and then signed at the formal closing where the business is formally transferred to the purchasing party. In some instances, business purchases are similar to real estate transactions where the purchase agreement is signed, but closing scheduled for a later date. In such instances, there are even fewer documents to sign at closing, with the primary issue being the compliance with closing covenants and conditions by the parties.

After the closing, the transaction attorney will work with the seller to assist in the filing or securing of any security interests pledged as part of the transaction, changing the selling entity's name (if the corporate name was purchased), collecting receivables, shutting down or dissolving the selling entity, and addressing any post-closing issues relating to employment, litigation, tax or related matters. As many purchase agreements provide that the seller will provide some sort of ongoing consultation or training, it is important for the parties to understand and negotiate the parameters of such post-closing involvement or training so perceived misunderstandings can be avoided. To the extent there are any post-closing disputes, the transaction attorney can assist in their negotiations and resolutions. Hopefully, the only post-closing contact between the sellers and the transaction attorney will be the formation of a new and unrelated successful business venture.

Following the closing of the transaction, your attorney should provide you with a neatly organized "deal book" which will contain copies of all pertinent documents and attachments. This information should be kept with the other documents referenced at the end of Chapter 5: Trusts and Estate Attorney.

Summary

The transaction attorney is an invaluable member of the seller's advisory team. Since the role of the attorney is so important to an efficient selling process, the seller should select a legal professional with expertise in mergers and acquisitions law and an understanding of what the seller *and* buyer need to conclude a successful transaction.

10 | From the Buyer's Perspective

WE'VE BEEN EXPLAINING HOW your M&A advisor guides you through the process of selling your business and what you need to do to maximize its value. We are at a point in the process where, once your CPA works through any questions brought up in the due diligence process and provides sufficient answers to the buyer's accountant, you may begin to see a light at the end of the tunnel.

Now, let's ask these simple, instructive questions: How does the buyer see this process? What is the buyer thinking about while assessing the value of your business?

Often it takes longer to close the deal than it does to find and qualify a buyer. There is good reason for this. We'll look at what the buyer wants and must have. This will clearly show why it can take longer to close the deal than to find the buyer.

A Buyer's Exit Strategy

You've heard the term before, most recently in the title of this book: Exit Strategy. As odd as it may sound, the buyer of your business is thinking about and planning his or her own exit strategy.

A buyer's purchase strategy begins with an exit strategy. Even before owning your business, the buyer is asking the following questions:

- ▸ Why do I want to buy a business?
- ▸ What kind of business am I going to buy?
- ▸ How am I going to improve profitability?
- ▸ How am I going to grow it?
- ▸ How long am I going to own it?
- ▸ How long will it take to get a return on my investment?
- ▸ How long will it take to get a return of my investment?
- ▸ When am I going to sell?
- ▸ What's my exit strategy?
- ▸ Who's going to buy it?
- ▸ How am I going to go about selling it?
- ▸ Will this provide enough money for the next stage my life?

In these questions you can see every topic covered in this book: financial and estate tax planning; a motivation for selling; valuing and preparing the business for sale; the role of an accountant and attorney; the need for an M&A advisor to define and guide the process. When a buyer buys, developing an exit strategy will be fundamental to purchasing your business.

Most business owners are too busy running businesses to have the time to fully develop an exit strategy. Does this sound like you? Probably, since 90 percent of business owners don't have a firm exit strategy in mind. And yet, the exit strategy is the basis of any buyer's purchase strategy.

The deal is made or not made based on the buyer's trust of the seller

The buyer will have his or her accountant analyze financial statements to make sure they're correct and conform to accounting standards. The accountant will study your financial statements to assess the margins and revenue.

At this stage of the selling process, the accountant is looking for large or unexplainable accounting variances and opportunities for improvement.

A Buyer's Due Diligence

Once you and the buyer agree on the letter of intent or the purchase agreement, the buyer and his or her accountant will begin the due diligence process. This provides the buyer with all the information needed to know what business is being acquired, what's involved in running it and what the "edge" or competitive advantage may be.

An accountant experienced in the M&A arena will search through every detail of the company, financial and otherwise. He or she will strive to answer hundreds of questions focused on an objective assessment of the viability of the business

For example, each business owner has an individual capital structure that must be analyzed by the buyer. A business' capital structure may include: banks, SBA loans, working lines of credit and equipment financing. When an owner sells his or her business, the existing capital structure must be unwound and the business prepared for a new structure. That may mean UCC filings to release any existing liens, proof of satisfaction of mortgages, title transfer notifications for leasing companies, among others.

The buyer's new capital structure will follow the business plan developed during the due diligence process.

As such, most of the due diligence process is education and fact-finding. If something comes up for question, the buyer will ask about it. And a sophisticated buyer won't stop asking questions about it until he or she understands the business as well as you.

The following points are brief summaries of what the buyer is working toward:

▶ First, the buyer is learning about the company and confirming that everything is as advertised.

▶ Second, the buyer is preparing for the closing by determining how to transfer all the assets being purchased.

▶ Third, the buyer is building confidence that he or she understands the business, knows how to operate it and knows what to do once it's purchased.

Due Diligence Topics

The due diligence process can be expensive for the buyer. From the buyer's perspective, however, thousands in due diligence fees is less expensive than buying a business that ends up losing money.

Generally speaking, the due diligence will cover the following topics:

General Inquiries This topic includes questions about your reason for selling and past and future market trends. It might include reading your annual and quarterly financial information and discussing that information with you, your company controller or the CFO.

History/Background of the Company The buyer will ask about the history of your business. It will include information such as your fiscal year, major stockholders, partners and owners, and what assumptions and goals you have created for your business and employees, among other information.

Industry This topic covers a broad spectrum of industry information. For example, it will include a description of your industry and an assessment of whether it is growing, declining or stable, major players, competitors, etc.

Management/Workforce The buyer will request an organizational chart and résumés for key employees. In looking at every aspect of the business, the buyer will make an assessment about the need for existing employees. You may have assembled the best management team and the best team of employees you thought possible. And, indeed, they may be. The buyer will make his or her own determination.

The buyer will assess whether the employees are self-starters and whether they're overpaid or underpaid. This involves an employee assessment. The buyer may or may not hire back all employees. And like all aspects of selling a business, the issue of employees may be subject to negotiation.

Products/Services and Pricing   The buyer will assess whether your pricing is reasonable and whether your margins are adequate. He or she will compare your margins to industry averages and will prepare a list of potential new products, products under development and discontinued products.

Accounting Principles and Practices   The accountant will conduct a thorough audit of the last 3 years' financial statements. He or she will look at the financials and footnotes first, to find out if they make sense and conform to accounting standards. The accountant will point out to the buyer any areas of concern.

Internal Control   This topic assesses whether you and your management team conveyed a sense of control consciousness to your personnel. That includes accounting controls and also covers hiring, supervising and following procedures, among many others. It also includes management's ability to override those controls under certain situations.

Sales   The buyer's accountant will conduct a comprehensive audit of your sales structure. He or she will look at your sales structure from various perspectives and will generate summaries that show trends, fluctuations, sales agreements, significant or unusual revenue or costs and various other topics. The accountant will confirm that sales are verified by your bank statements and in balance with your financial statements.

Customer Base   A comprehensive list will be prepared assessing your major customers, sales, profitability or gross margin.

Accounts Receivable   The buyer will want to control any outstanding receivables in order to control the customer relationship.

Sales Force, Marketing and The buyer will prepare a summary of
Distribution Methods your sales force and marketing structure, including individual sales perfor-
mances, compensation structure and marketing and advertising costs,
among other topics. The buyer will review descriptions of your distribution methods, any agreements with distributors, transportation used for
distribution and payment terms for shipping.

Transactions With The accountant will prepare a list of
Related Parties related parties and transactions, such
as transactions with subsidiaries, "sis-
ter companies" and other affiliated companies, partnerships or joint
ventures.

Inventory Often, existing inventory will need to be
analyzed and negotiated. Some of it
may be obsolete and of no value to the buyer.

Cost of Goods Sold The accountant will prepare a summary of cost of goods sold and gross prof-
it for recent periods and will inquire concerning the cause of any trends
or fluctuations noted.

Operating Expenses Not only do they analyze your operating expenses, but they will compare
them to others in the industry and assess your efficiency. They will
analyze every single expense in order to understand your overhead
costs.

The accountant will verify payment records and pricing of inventory. In a manufacturing situation, the accountant will review your time and
expense studies showing how much time, money and material you have
in each part and assess whether the part is priced correctly.

Remember, the buyer is trying to find a competitive edge, a way to
maximize the profitability of the business going forward.

Prepaids, Deferred Charges, The accountant will want schedules
Intangibles, Investments of prepaid assets, deferred charges,
and Other Assets intangible assets, accounts payable,
accrued expenses and deferred rev-
enue and other assets.

Income Tax Liabilities The accountant helps the buyer analyze the income tax issues and how
they really affect the bottom line. What kind of tax has the seller been
paying? The accountant will get a sense of the big picture. There may be
deductions that owners take for tax purposes that rightly could be added
into the profit statement; deductions such as: accelerated depreciation,
or bonus depreciation that may be unrelated to the life of the assets.

In a stock purchase, it's even more important for a buyer to have an
accountant audit the business' tax returns and assess tax payments or
due tax. Even if you agree to warranties and representations regarding
taxes and other financial statements, because it's a stock sale, taxing
authorities would seek out the current owner first. Even if ultimately you
take responsibility for making past-due payments, the buyer will be
involved.

Under a stock purchase deal, the buyer will go to a lot more work to
feel comfortable that all liabilities and potential liabilities are accounted
for and paid in full.

Commitments and The buyer's lawyer will ask whether
Contingencies you're currently involved in any litigation. Have you been involved in any in
the past? Are there any outstanding commitments or contingencies
based on that or other litigation? Is there a history of litigation? Does
this affect the business going forward?

Land and Buildings The accountant and buyer will want to
tour your offices and production facili-
ties to observe their age and condition. They will assess whether they
want to lease or buy the property.

Cash and The accountant will prepare a list
Equivalencies cash accounts, equivalents and bal-
ances.

Notes Payable and Long-Term Debt   These will be recorded to ensure that seller obligations are taken care of.

Equity   The accountant will want a description of your legal structure. The accountant may ask to see the corporate charter, articles of incorporation, bylaws, partnership agreements, etc.

Insurance   The buyer's accountant and transaction attorney will ask about insurance and workers' compensation rates. They will raise liability issues about auto insurance and employee life insurance. The buyer will want to be released from any liability for occurrences linked to the seller's ownership of the business.

Employee Benefit Plans   The buyer will want a thorough description of all employee benefit plans, including any retirement programs currently in place.

Information Systems   The buyer and his or her accountant will assess the kind of computers and software you use. They will look at whether or not you've been paying your software license fees and will consider the age, size and speed of the hardware. They will then try to determine if it is adequate for future growth.

Environmental Issues   The buyer will look at what you've done with environmental waste. They'll want proof that it was disposed of legally and that no issues remain.

Intellectual Property   The buyer and his or her accountant will list and assess trademark registrations, copyrights and proprietary registrations.

Finally, the buyer will want to meet you and assess whether he or she can trust you. All deals ultimately depend on the bond of trust built between you and the buyer.

The above listing is only a brief summary of each topic. In actuality, the buyer and an accountant will ask about everything that has happened in your business under your ownership. They will want to see every document — and all the problems and challenges, the good and the bad.

The buyer is looking to understand what the business is and that it is consistent with how it was presented. The buyer wants to confirm that the business plan being developed to operate your business profitably is sound.

The Seller's Role in the Buyer's Success

You can safely bet that part of the buyer's plan is to realize a return of the investment as well as a return on the investment. As the seller you have a stake in helping the buyer realize these investment goals.

The buyer's investment will generally come down two main avenues: Part One will be personal investment, or down payment. Part Two will be the financed portion of the acquisition debt. That return can be defined in three parts:

▸ Return of investment (the buyer wants the investment back as soon as possible)

▸ Return on investment (the buyer may expect a return of 15 to 20 percent or more on the investment)

▸ Financed portion to be paid from the business' cash flow

For most buyers, the test is this: If the bank debt can be paid off in a reasonable number of years and, in the same time, get a return on the investment and a return of the investment — typically within five to seven years — the business was probably valued accurately. If it takes the buyer 10 or 15 years to achieve those goals, probably too much was paid.

From the buyer's perspective, the ideal business to purchase is where the seller does nothing but come to board meetings; the CFO compiles the financial documents and you simply read them. The president or CEO is active in all parts of the business, and all executives or managers are active and in control of their respective duties. The more you can systematize things and compartmentalize things, the better. This tells the buyer that the business operates more or less independently of you. The buyer takes your place and the business will continue as it has.

Unfortunately, that's the ideal situation. The buyer will assess whether his or her business goals can be achieved without you. A buyer probably will want you to stick around for some period of time (usually at least one full business cycle) to help ensure that the business continues to operate efficiently and profitably.

Ultimately, your success in selling and walking away from your business clean and clear of any liability is dependent on the buyer's success. Therefore, it is in your best interests to help the buyer by answering questions honestly and helping the buyer achieve all stated goals.

Now that you have an understanding of what the buyer is thinking about, let's move on to the last part of the process of selling your business. ■

11 | Negotiating and Closing the Deal

THE M&A ADVISOR WILL negotiate the sale agreement on your behalf in the best manner possible to achieve your wishes. Negotiation is a continuous process that brings a buyer and seller together in order to complete the sale. Negotiations should be reasonable and don't have to be hostile; but recognizing that every deal has two sides or perspectives, compromise must be found. Good negotiations seek compromises that provide each party with their desired benefits. And at this stage, you should be prepared to make decisions throughout the process of selling your business.

The subtleties of negotiation happen every step of the way

The M&A advisor will negotiate based on advice from you and your advisory team. This may include negotiating a letter of intent, purchase agreement, buy/sell agreement, consulting agreement, employment agreements and non-compete agreements. Each deal will include negotiations for the structure of the sale; price and terms; real estate; intangible assets; allocating the purchase price; and anything else the buyer or seller have to work out.

It is the M&A advisor's responsibility to keep the transaction moving forward at all times and to coordinate involvement of the advisory team on your behalf in order to complete the transaction in a timely fashion.

Buyers and Values

Multiple buyers may offer to purchase your business under different structures and for different amounts. One buyer may want a stock purchase. Another buyer may be interested in an asset purchase. A third may not want the real estate, but everything else. Your M&A advisor and team will assess the offers, determine which is in your best interest and then explain how each offer either fits or doesn't fit your financial strategy. This complete assessment of multiple offers will help you make the best decision about whom to deal with.

At some point, the buyers will provide an estimate of value, or a ballpark value. Working with your M&A advisor, you will pick two or three buyers who have given the most reasonable value and fit the criteria of a serious buyer. Having chosen serious buyers to deal with, your advisor schedules a management presentation with them. Every presentation is different. Typically they include a tour of the facility, a meeting with you and your management team and a discussion about the business.

As discussed in Chapter Nine, much of the negotiations involve the letter of intent and the purchase agreement. The content of the deal as set forth in the letter of intent can and probably will change by the time you close the deal.

With a signed letter of intent, we remove your business from the market and proceed toward a purchase agreement. As the buyer and his or her advisors conduct due diligence, they may use whatever they find to try to negotiate a lower price or better terms. You will need your team to advise you on the best way to respond to each issue. Your CPA and transaction attorney may truly have a chance to show their expertise.

Your Advisors and Negotiation

While experience is essential, you will discover that closing the deal may take skill in finding compromise. Your team of professionals—and particularly your M&A advisor, CPA and M&A attorney—will help find the middle ground that satisfies you and the buyer.

During the due diligence process, the buyer will discover aspects of your business about which he or she will comment: "Well, that's not what I expected." Or, "That piece of equipment is not what I thought." The buyer will present an assessment of your business one way; you will respond in another. Compromise will be needed. Coordinated by your M&A advisor, your team will respond to these and other points of negotiation.

The M&A advisor will conduct a meeting with you, your CPA and other advisors as needed. He or she will have your CPA or attorney explain the buyer's offer or points of negotiation and will make sure that all options on how to respond and their ramifications for you have been explained. Then, you will decide how to respond and you will direct your M&A advisor to negotiate for that purpose or goal.

At some point in the process, the lead in negotiation may shift to the M&A attorney. Your attorney and the buyer's attorney will negotiate the details of the language of the deal. Your attorney will keep you and your M&A advisor informed of progress and details at all times.

Closing the Deal

The M&A advisor will help facilitate the closing of the deal. This includes assisting in the delivery of documents, titles, copies of vendor agreements and all other items necessary to satisfy the attorneys so that the closing of the transaction can take place in a timely and efficient manner. If all information necessary to close the deal is delivered early, it may be possible to have an uneventful and friendly closing consisting of signing the documents and delivery of checks, promissory notes and other documents.

At the beginning of this book, we said that preparing your business for sale is a process and that the more prepared you are, the easier it would be to negotiate and close the deal. At this stage of the selling process you will begin to see the results of preparing your business for sale.

There will be obstacles and each must be dealt with, so there's no point in putting it off. An experienced M&A advisor may anticipate the obstacles and help remove them before they disrupt the deal. The closing will happen as soon as the parties have eliminated all the obstacles.

The quickest way to close a deal is to remove all of the obstacles

If your M&A advisor presents your business as completely as possible, dealing only with the facts and trying to shine the best light possible on them, then you'll encounter few surprises, and they should be small ones.

Both sides have concerns and needs that must be addressed. Closing the deal means removing the obstacles so that both parties feel comfortable about signing the documents.

Building Trust

Nothing helps close the deal like building trust between you and the buyer. When the buyer trusts you and is comfortable talking with you about the business, then obstacles tend to become minor tasks instead of potential deal breakers.

We encourage the seller and buyer to spend time together talking about the history of the business. You should tell the buyer why you made certain decisions and why certain efforts succeeded while others failed. Discuss the history of the industry and the business' place in that history.

Listen to the buyer's ideas about how to make your business more profitable. If you've already tried some of the ideas, then explain how you went

At some point in the process, every one of our clients comes to what can be a frightening realization: "I'm really selling my business!" This is seller's remorse

about implementing them and why they worked or didn't work. Listen for any concerns the buyer may have and, while it won't be your sole responsibility to alleviate those concerns, you can make some suggestions based on your industry knowledge and expertise.

And be sure to answer the buyer's questions. Spend time explaining your answers until the buyer is satisfied. Building trust between you and the buyer is essential to closing the deal successfully.

A Smooth Finish

In the last hours of the deal, the attorneys put final details into the purchase agreement. By closing time, both sides have seen all the documents and the buyer is prepared to wire funds into your account. To bring the process to closure smoothly, both you and the buyer must clearly and thoroughly understand the purchase agreement. This is important because if there is a problem after the closing, the parties will turn to the purchase agreement to resolve it.

The actual closing event tends to be anticlimactic.

During the transition period, you may become emotional — frustrated or even angry — because you're not calling the shots. Month by month, the new president asks fewer and fewer questions. You will become less and less key to the operation and profitability of the business. It could be particularly shocking when six months into your contract the buyer informs you that you're no longer needed on a daily basis. The buyer may pay you what remains on your contract and tell you, "We'll call if we need anything."

This can be traumatic and you need to be prepared to move on with your life. Just because you no longer run the business you started, built and ran for many years, it doesn't mean that life is over and your worth in the world is diminished. If anything, the opposite is true. You have built and sold a successful business. You have a lot to offer the world; it just isn't through the entity of your business. Besides that, you got a truckload of wealth. Cash flow is no longer your Friday afternoon concern; the buyer can worry about that. You can move on with fewer worries!

This is a time for new beginnings; the world is filled with unique and compelling opportunities. It's time to explore the world and discover new meanings for your life.

What to Do With All Those Documents?

Now that you've finally finished up the deal, what do you do with all of this paperwork?

This is an opportune time to organize your important paperwork and file it securely in a safe deposit box or a fireproof safe at home. Your transaction attorney will provide you with a closing book, which will contain copies of all of the documents that were necessary to close the sale of your business. Your trusts and estate attorney will have given you an organized folder of materials containing your will, trust documents and all other relevant documents outlining your affairs. Your financial planner will have given you some detailed paperwork, projections and plan documents regarding the financial decisions you have made during the process.

This is also a good time to finish the job of detailing the other personal and financial information in your life that you deem important. Much of this may already have been organized during your estate planning activities. (See: "Trusts and Estate Attorney") You may want to keep these documents current by reviewing and updating them, periodically (perhaps on an annual basis).

Taking the time to completely organize your personal and financial information will prove to be valuable in keeping your affairs in order and will also serve as a road map for your spouse or personal representative later in life. You may want to let your attorney, spouse and children know where to look for the information, in case it is needed. ∎

12 | Selling a Professional Practice

BUYING AND SELLING a professional practice is somewhat different because the change in ownership is quite often done internally. However, an experienced and talented CPA and transaction attorney are still fundamental to a successful deal.

Often, an interest in a professional practice will be sold internally to a partner or shareholder of the firm. In these cases, the seller identifies, recruits and develops a younger associate, or associates with the thought that one or more of them will eventually become a partner and buy out retiring partners when appropriate.

If the seller decides to search outside the firm for a buyer, then an M&A advisor can identify other firms looking to grow or expand by acquisition into the seller's geographic area. M&A advisors can quarterback the selling process. An experienced M&A advisor will help you to negotiate the sale of the practice, keeping you at arm's length from the buyer until you are ready to proceed.

Employee Stock Option Plans, or ESOPS, are another way of passing along ownership of a professional practice. ESOPS allow the owner to distribute stock to employees as a form of compensation. In exchange, the owner gains certain tax advantages.

There are about 11,000 ESOPS in the United States; of these, 95 percent are closely held firms. About half are used for the purpose of buying out the current owner. To find out if an ESOP may be an effective part of your exit strategy, contact your CPA or an attorney specializing in ESOPs.

The remainder of this chapter discusses issues included in selling a professional practice both internally and externally. Many issues are similar.

Valuing the Practice

Most professional practices distribute their earnings annually and retain minimal assets. Their balance sheets typically reflect only limited assets and liabilities due to the distributions. When buying into a service business or a professional practice, the market value of the hard assets is going to be minimal in most cases. Much of the value of this type of company will come from the relationships with the clients, reputation of the firm and intangibles such as patents, copyrights, books and other materials developed by the partners. This value is commonly referred to as goodwill or blue sky.

As compared to other businesses, most professional practices sell "internally" and are based upon a formula and subject to a buy/sell agreement; or "externally" with a small fixed price based upon hard assets and an earn-out based upon client retention and earnings.

Internal Sale An internal sale of a professional practice involves associates of the firm who are already working with the clients and developing relationships. Because they are already so involved in the business, they are usually willing to purchase it, or part of it, based upon a fixed valuation formula and a buy/sell agreement; often this includes plans to buy out retiring partners in the future based on stock redemption and deferred compensation agreements that are carefully planned with attorneys, CPAs, and other partners of the firm.

These associates will know everything necessary to assume ownership with confidence in the current condition of the business. They know the firm's credit history, cash flow matters and key clients, among other important business issues. They also understand the firm's culture, character, work ethic, and other aspects that help make them comfortable and confident buyers. In essence, they have lived the due diligence process and are prepared to take over the reigns of leadership with very few changes.

In this scenario, it is important to understand that young partners may not have the money to pay for the purchase in cash, and that you will have to find ways to facilitate their purchase of an interest in the practice. This can be accomplished with offsets to future income, long-term promissory notes, adjustments to capital accounts and agreement to take on obligations to the retiring or departing partners in conjunction with their buyout arrangements. Each practice will have to find an acceptable method of accommodating new and departing partners to enable the practice to continue in a profitable manor.

External Sale   When an owner of a professional practice is unsuccessful in recruiting a partner to take over the firm or unable to do so, he or she may sell it to an external buyer; that is, someone from "outside" the firm.

The structure at the time of closing an external sale commonly consists of a limited amount of cash paid to the seller, with the remainder of the value paid through an earn-out over a negotiated period of time.

An earn-out limits the inherent risks involved in buying a professional practice from outside the firm. It can do so by calculating a large portion of the purchase price based upon the buyer's ability to keep the firm's current clients and continuing the income stream. This also provides a direct monetary incentive for the seller to help keep clients satisfied and retain them for the firm.

Going outside the firm to sell may bring a higher price, but it also may bring more risk for the buyer. Under these circumstances, the buyer will want to thoroughly investigate every aspect of the seller's business. This begins a due diligence process in which the buyer comes to trust the seller and understand the business.

Due diligence for an external sale often takes longer and is more involved than that of an internal sale. This is because the external buyer knows little about the firm being purchased, whereas the internal buyer has the advantage of having worked at the firm and developing client relationships.

During due diligence the external buyer learns in-depth information about the business being purchased. A sophisticated buyer will ask questions about the business until he or she understands it completely.

This is a time for the seller to develop a relationship with the buyer, being completely open and explaining every aspect of the business. As with any investment, the more the buyer knows about the business will improve his or her comfort level with the deal and increase the opportunity to close the deal.

See "From The Buyer's Perspective," for a comprehensive discussion of due diligence.

As you can see from the discussions of an internal or external sale, the differing degree of risk will have a direct affect on the cash received at the closing and the total amount received for the sale of the practice. Even riskier would be a situation where a practice would sell to a public firm using mostly stock, with some cash, to purchase a practice. In this type of sale, sometimes referred to as a "roll up", when multiple purchases are being made by the buying entity, the chances of the buyer failing to take care of the client relationships is much greater than internal sales and should be contemplated when trying to gauge the future value of the stock received at the sale. Be sure that you and your advisors do a proper risk assessment of this type of transaction prior to entering into any agreements.

Buy/Sell Agreements, Valuations & Formulas

Buy/sell agreements are formalized agreements among owners that are designed to protect the business with first rights of refusal from unexpected eventualities, such as voluntary retirement, involuntary retirement or death of any of the partners. Buy/sell agreements may place restrictions on stock sales requiring them to be offered to the company or other partners before selling outside the business; and they will usually place a timeline on the acceptance of such offers.

The value, terms and timing of the sale are normally dictated in the buy/sell agreement. Typically, these are favorable terms for the buyer.

Stockholders at their annual meetings sometimes establish valuation issues in buy/sell agreements. Stockholders may assign a value for stock for a period of time, one year, for example. Or, they may agree on a set formula that develops the value of the stock, based upon financial statements at some future date. Alternatively, a firm may elect to use periodic independent valuations to establish value in conjunction with a defined benefit plan, both of which will be based upon the assumption that the practice will continue in the future by adding new partners to constantly replace the departing or retiring partners.

These valuation discussions can be further complicated when contemplating the case of a departing partner who takes clients with him at the time he leaves the practice. Offsets in the amount owed to the departing partner, because of the loss of a portion of the client base, will have to be taken into account when calculating capital accounts, stock values and deferred compensation. These and other issues can be anticipated during the drafting of the buy/sell agreements, if you are doing so with the help of an experienced attorney.

A buy/sell agreement may include life insurance provisions for each partner. In the event that one partner dies, the insurance may be used to purchase his or her share of the business from the estate. Speak with your financial planner or insurance agent about the best way to own this insurance.

A possible inclusion to a buy/sell agreement is a clause stating that if one partner approaches another partner with a request to buy him or her out, the second partner may decline and turn the sale around, forcing the first partner to sell his or her shares to the second for the same terms offered. This clause is meant to assure that any sale among partners is fair and equitable by assuring that the first partner values the business correctly.

A thorough discussion of typical buy/sell provisions with an experienced corporate attorney should be a part of the process of developing an exit strategy for your practice.

Cross Indemnification Agreement

Bank financing or lines of credit may require personal guarantees. If the firm defaults, the bank will go after the deepest pockets, often that is the senior partner. To get the money reimbursed from the other partners, the senior partner may have to litigate. Cross indemnification agreements remind all partners that they are responsible for liabilities to the extent of their ownership interest; and they protect all partners from liabilities greater than their percentages of ownership in the business. Speak with your attorney for more information about cross indemnification agreements.

Key Employees & Non-compete Agreements

Regardless of whether it is an internal or external sale, key employees are critical to the continued success and profitability of the professional practice. A buyer of the firm will want some assurance that key employees will stay with the business after he or she assumes ownership, to manage key accounts and continue a smooth operation. A buyer may require employment agreements for key employees.

The buyer of a professional practice will want also assurance that the sellers or their key employees will not damage the business by joining a competing firm or establishing a new practice. This assurance may take the form or a non-compete agreement. Discuss the terms of a non-compete with your attorney to determine what may or may not be enforceable.

Risk Management

Even after the sale of your professional practice, you still may be liable for certain risks associated with the practice. Such risks can be protected against with the use of warranties and representations and tail insurance coverage. Consult with your attorney in order to identify and account for residual risks associated with the sale of your practice prior to signing any documents.

Regulatory Oversight

When selling, research the guidelines and rules established by any professional oversight body governing your profession.

For instance, lawyers in Minnesota have the board of professional responsibility, which regulates law firms and the use of their trust funds and imposes a requirement of being an attorney to hold an interest in a professional legal practice.

Until recently, partners of CPA firms were required to be a CPA. As the accounting profession has expanded into other services, firms may now be allowed to have non-CPA partners in those specific areas.

The regulatory authority governing the profession involved may have additional restrictions concerning who can and cannot own the shares of a professional service organization. These rules may be different from state to state. Consult your attorney about all aspects of ownership in a professional practice before buying or selling.

Summary

Professional practices, such as legal, accounting, engineering, architectural medical or dental practices, may sell a bit differently than a manufacturing or distribution company. This is due to the nature of a service business that places most of the value on client relationships and the ability to maintain them following a change in ownership of the practice. Because of the risk that the business may disappear with the seller, the price paid for the practice will reflect the buyer's level of confidence in holding the business together, post sale. ■

Epilogue: After the Sale: What Then? Successful Retirement Requires Planning

THIS CHAPTER WAS WRITTEN with generous contributions of time and expertise by Richard Christison.

Richard Christison bought his first business, a newspaper in Michigan, when he was 26. He sold that business after he had become managing partner in the advertising agency Coleman & Christison. For over 20 years he ran the ad agency, a governmental affairs agency and a graphic arts firm, before selling them all and becoming "semi-retired." He has been a confidant of Mr. Lyons since they created the first advertising for a law firm in the Twin Cities. Today, Mr. Christison travels, consults, mentors and has fun.

So you've done it. You've sold your business and are starting a new life. But how are you going to spend your time when you don't have to worry about customer service? What are you going to think about when you don't have vendor, delivery people or person-

For some entrepreneurs, selling their business is indeed "free at last"—a lifting of the many burdens of running a business. But most entrepreneurs never look on the multiple tasks of running a business as being burdens. Most entrepreneurs enjoy the challenges of solving problems every day.

You've been good at a lot of different kinds of tasks. What will you do to replace the stimulation of business—the joys of doing important things well?

Whether it's providing extra value for a long-term customer or negotiating a better deal from a vendor, an entrepreneur has a wide variety of potentially satisfying situations every day.

And, since you were good at building and running your business, you've shown that you're good at a lot of different kinds of tasks. Whether you know it or not, you've been on a diet of personal positive reinforcement, and that diet has now come to an end. So what are you going to do with yourself? What will you do to replace the stimulation of business—the joys of doing important things well, the pleasure of solving puzzles?

If you're someone who has always made time for family and community, has a variety of interests and hobbies, enjoys learning new things and going new places, then get ready to enjoy the rest of your life. Because now, with the sale of your business, you'll have the time and money to continue doing the things you love.

But if you're like most entrepreneurs, you've focused most of your time and energy on your business. And now you are going to have to create a new life, and you're going to have to do some serious thinking about who and what you want to be. You're about to enter a time of your life that you may be totally unprepared for.

Building Your Post Business Life

It's up to you to define what your new status will be. Are you retired? Semi-retired? Between businesses? Looking for a new career? You have a lot of options—but sitting around watching daytime television shouldn't be one of them. You must remain active,

If you are going to retire, this new phase of your life is probably going to last longer than you thought. It used to be that when people retired, they had already lived much of their life. But earlier retirements combined with longer life spans have most retirees living about half as long as they were working. In fact, if you had retired in 1970, you probably had worked 45 years and had 13 years left to live. But at the turn of the twenty-first century, the number of years worked had dropped to 42 and the number of years in retirement had increased to 18, according to government statistics. You might be even younger than average. The sale of your business will probably provide you the money you need for this longer period, but it's up to you to figure out what you want to do.

You're about to enter a time of your life for which you may be totally unprepared

Time to Take Inventory

The first thing to do is take your personal inventory. What do you like to do? What things have you regretted not doing? What's important to you? What would you like to be known for? Where would you like to go?

The easiest way to do this is simply start a two-column list with these headings: "What do I like to do?" and "What's important to me?"

It's time to identify what you like to do and what's important to you. Start a list, and then bring your list to life

In the first column might be fishing, golf, travel, food, boating, skiing, hiking—whatever you like to do, write it down. And don't just stop at three or four items; if you like something, or used to like something, write it down.

If you need some inspiration, go to the magazine section of a major bookstore. You'll find magazines on almost anything you've ever thought of doing—something as simple as walking has several magazines. And, if you're still stumped for ideas of what to do, go to various hobbies. And that's not counting the 12,000 groups devoted to collecting, or the thousands of groups for recreational activities.

Next comes the fun part. Starting with the things you like to do, take each item and expand on it. If you listed golf, then think of all the ways to expand on the pleasure of golf: lessons from pros in North Carolina, a golf cruise through the Caribbean, playing St. Andrews—the only limit is your imagination. If you're interested in genealogy, then visit the courthouses and cemeteries where your ancestors lived. If you like wine, plan a visit to wineries in the United States, France, Italy, Spain—or maybe even Chili, Argentina or Australia. Or start making your own wine—grapes grow, and can ferment, anywhere in America. If you like good food, discover spectacular cooking schools nearby or at a distance.

As you set your personal goals, they should set a personal record for you, a record of retirement pleasure

When you're creating your list of potential projects, if you can come up with only two or three things, ask some friends to help out. Each item listed should yield a half-dozen potential adventures.

You wouldn't be the first person to buy an RV and go off to fish in every one of the lower 48 states, golf at every public course within 1,000 miles, or canoe in every river in the state. Of course, your goal here doesn't have to set any world record. But it should set a personal record for you, a record of retirement pleasure. Just be certain your list includes activities that are active—walking, hiking, skiing, dancing, golfing, etc., are all activities that need to be included. You need to do things that are fun, but stay active. Health clubs make exercise easier, as do personal trainers. But the easiest way to stay active is to do things you enjoy.

As you list the areas of potential fun, you might want to consider a part-time job in one of the areas. Even if you don't need the money, having a part-time job ensures you constant contact with other people and a chance to be involved with something you like. Driving ranges need help, as do gardening centers, book stores, resorts, colleges, etc. As a part-time worker you won't get any benefits, but you wouldn't have them anyway.

The items of importance to you are easier. If something's important, what can you do to help? If it's grandchildren, then budget time for them. Make certain that the time you spend is, to the extent possible, memorable. Create memories for them as you're enjoying yourself with them. If at all possible, get your grandkids away from their parents for a break — for a day, a week or a month.

If you've listed a charity as being important, you can volunteer time or contribute money. There's going to be at least one thing you can do for every item of importance. Perhaps you've created a charitable trust or foundation (see Chapter Five) and now you need to ensure its stability. Time spent evaluating requests for funding can be fulfilling.

A quick note on volunteering: If you haven't done much volunteer work before, you'll discover that there are as many volunteer positions as there are working jobs. You can pick a cause you like and see how your skills fit their needs (if you like the Cancer Society, meet with their volunteer coordinator and see how well you fit). Or, you can decide what you want to do and go looking for a non-profit — if you like antiques, then perhaps you can spend some time at a non-profit consignment shop, for example. Or, if you want to do some financial planning, many organizations can use your help. Many local newspapers have a "volunteers needed" section (if your newspaper doesn't have one, ask them to add it). Volunteers of America (www.voa.org) can help match you to a cause that takes advantage of your skills.

Your list can include lots of things: hobbies, travel, sports, volunteering and part-time jobs. The only thing it can't include is inactivity

Before you prioritize these potential projects, ask your spouse for input. (Now that you're retired, your spouse takes on the additional title of Managing Partner. And remember, without a business life your personal life is your only life. So be very good to the Managing Partner.) And if you find out that your spouse has been waiting 25 years to visit relatives in Norway, then it's obvious that your golf outing is going to have to wait for a while.

With your spouse's assistance, prioritize the potential projects. Iinclude both the fun things and the important things. Then take the first five or six items on your lists and set dates for them. For the next six months, see how many you can accomplish. You're set to go.

Join AARP — They Can Help You

Since you are now part of the most important demographic group around (not only are the retirees growing in number, but they also admit you're getting older. But now's the time to start accepting and enjoying your new status.have much of the money), there are a number of places you can turn to for help. The first place to go, if you haven't already, is to join AARP. Perhaps you've delayed joining because you were hesitant to admit you're getting older. But now's the time to start accepting and enjoying your new status.

For a few dollars a year, you'll receive a host of benefits and access to exactly the kind of information you want. Save money on travel, insurance, legal care — it's the kind of benefit you deserve. You can contact them at www.aarp.org, or call 1-888-687-2277. They'll help keep you active and save you money.

Mentoring Opportunities

If you would still like to stay involved with the business world and don't need a paycheck, there are several great places to volunteer. One of the best known is the Service Corps of Retired Executives (SCORE). You can contact them at www.score.org, or call 1-800-634-0245. This group of savvy former businesspeople helps small businesses with the advice and consulting that experience provides.

Another such group, with some adventure thrown in, is Citizens Development Corps (formerly Citizens Democracy Corps) (CDC). You can contact them at www.cdc.org, or call 1-202-872-0933. This group sends experienced businesspeople to work with businesses in developing countries. How does two months in Thailand, or a month in Russia, sound to you? You might be able to really make a difference, and gain the satisfaction of success, in a foreign land.

If you want to help someone but don't want to leave your desk, then there's a new program designed for you. MicroMentor, a project of the Aspen Institute, matches startup companies (protégés) with experienced businesspeople (mentors). You can contact them at www.micromentor.org, or call 1-503-465-4181. You commit to answering emails from your protégé to help them get started. It's an exciting program with lots of positive results.

Whatever you do after you leave business, you should first congratulate yourself and those around you. You're a winner. You now have some great choices to make, some wonderful time to spend. Help others, help yourself, and have fun. Mostly have fun. ∎

In Closing...

Now that you know how to maximize the value before selling your business and the role of an M&A advisor, here are a few thoughts about selecting one. These thoughts are based on decades of experience and on how the advisors at my firm, Faelon Partners, Ltd. approach our clientele.

First, the M&A advisor you choose should be familiar with every aspect of this book, from the selling process itself to the roles of each advisor to recognizing and resolving obstacles to advance the close of the sale.

Second, the M&A advisor you choose to work with should have extensive experience across multiple industries and have access to the many possible buyers of your business.

Finally, and perhaps most importantly, you must be comfortable sharing a lot of confidential information with your M&A advisor. Throughout the process of defining and selling your business, he or she will learn more about your business than any other individual involved. In the course of telephone conversations, lunches and an array of meetings with other professionals and potential buyers, you will find your M&A advisor to be a valued confidant. The nature of the selling process often produces a lasting friendship between you and your advisor.

The process laid out in this book is what a seller can expect from Faelon Partners, Ltd.: the scope is full-service and broad-based. Because not all firms service their clients in the same way, it is important to discuss the engagement in detail with the M&A advisor and require an engagement letter that states clearly what services will be performed and what fees will be charged.

The process of selling your business can be complex, but you don't have to do it alone. As this book has explained, the M&A advisor can be your guide and facilitate the selling process. The M&A advisor will help you utilize the valuable advice of your financial planner, attorneys and CPAs and will help implement the informed decisions you have made in order to successfully sell your business.

So, if you are ready to sell, call Faelon Partners, Ltd. With Faelon serving as your M&A firm, we will gather your team around you and put them in a position to help you maximize the value of your business.

Faelon Partners, Ltd. can be reached by calling 763-231-4200 Ext.1. Or find us on the Web at www.faelon.com.

What Business Owners and Advisors Are Saying About *Exit $trategy*

I am convinced that without implementing the strategy outlined in Exit Strategy, a seller would lose 30% to 40% of the money they deserve from the sale of their business.

    George Abraham, President, Business Evaluation Systems

I highly recommend Exit Strategy for anyone who will be involved in buying or selling a business. The management insights and practical skills presented in this book are extremely important in conducting negotiations successfully.

    Gary Rappaport, President, Venturian Corporation

Exit Strategy *so clearly identifies the planning that must occur long before a business owner is ready to sell. It's a very important and practical resource for business owners and their advisors.*

    Marjorie Mathison Hance, Vice President for External Relations and Co-founder, International Institute for Women Entrepreneurs, The College of St. Catherine

Businesses that follow Exity Strategy principles will find that they are more attractive candidates for private equity investors. The preparation, planning and execution outlined in Tom's book are paramount to maximizing the value of your business.

    Steve Soderling, Principal, Tonka Bay Equity Partners

As a businessman and financial advisor to business owners I understand the core issue. Trying to integrate business transition efforts into the day-to-day challenges of operating and growing a business requires additional information, time and decision making. If this is the first time a business owner has been through this effort it can at times feel like a daunting task. Tom's book takes the process and lays it out in a fashion that gives the reader an awareness of what is involved and a way to, perhaps, better outcomes.

Thomas Fee, Principal, Managing Partner, Vector Wealth Management

Tom Lyons' Exit Strategy *is a useful tool for business owners as they work to maximize the value of their businesses. The easy-to-follow format appeals to the practical-minded entrepreneur.*

Beth Ewen, Editor and co-founder, Upsize Minnesota Magazine.

After reading the book, I met Tom, found him to be a straight-up, no-nonsense kind of guy, so I bought copies for all of my members and told them each to read it five years before they intend to harvest.

Norm Stoehr, Founder & Chairman, Inner Circle

Since reading Exit Strategy, *I'm much more diligent in all my business growth plans because now I see where it's all going. It helps you understand the importance of knowing what you want out of your business and how you're going to get it. A wise exit strategy is an opportunity to leave a legacy for your children's children.*

Tom Kieffer, President, Lighting Masters

Exit Strategy emphasizes the importance of comprehensive professional M&A representation when preparing to exit a business. The book clearly explains how a team of professionals led by an M&A advisor can help business owners maximize the value of their businesses.

Thomas S. Gitis, Attorney at Law

Large businesses aren't the only ones that can benefit from reading Exit Strategy. *It's extremely helpful for $1-5 million and middle market companies, too.*

George Kinley, Owner, Kinley Golf & Sport

Exit Strategy is the kind of book you can't put down; you keep it nearby so you can always refer to it. It makes you think about life—family, wife, children, friendships—and how the sale of the business may affect them.

Jimmy Theros, Founder, St. Clair Broiler

Exit Strategy showed the importance of planning, preparation and timing to the sale of my business. The book's precepts greatly benefited me.

Joe Peltier, Founder, Crashedtoys.com

This book is an indispensable resource for all business owners and advisors. It should be read by anyone selling a business.

Dave Hoitomt, Vice President, M&I Bank (Retired)

As Exit Strategy *clearly explains, a CPA with M&A experience is an essential member of the advisory team necessary for selling a business. Reading this book will help many business owners utilize their CPAs to the fullest, and help to maximize their net after tax profit when they sell.*

David Peltz, CPA

I enjoyed Exit Strategy, *and can see it is a valuable tool for the small business owner.*

Curtis Bradford, Attorney at Law

Exit Strategy *should be read by anybody who's thinking about starting a business—because you need to know how to get out of it before you even get into it.*

Walt Wittmer, Founder, Builder & Former General Manager, Valley Fair Amusement Park

I wish I had read Exit Strategy *previous to starting my business. It would have helped me achieve my financial objectives sooner. I think everyone should read this book before starting a business.*

Kevin Hanson, Founder and President, Omega Lithograph

Printed in the United States
117650LV00004B/1-207/P